A PRESTON MIXTURE

Compiled by

Bob Dobson

Landy Publishing

2003

ISBN 1 872895 61 1

British Library in Cataloguing Publication Data
A catalogue record of the book is available from the British Library

Layout by CJD Tel : 01254 240267

Printed by Nayler The Printer, Church, Accrington. Tel 01254 234217

Published by Landy Publishing
"Acorns", 3 Staining Rise,
Staining, Blackpool FY3 0BU
Tel/Fax 01253 895678

Landy Publishing have also published:-
Northward by "Atticus" (Anthony Hewitson)
Preston in Focus by Stephen Sartin
Blackburn in Focus by Alan Duckworth & Jim Halsall
Cockersand Abbey by Brian Marshall
A Century of Bentham by David Johnson
Bygone Bentham by Joseph Carr
Accrington Public Transport by Robert Rush
Accrington's Changing Face by Frank Watson & Bob Dobson
Bolland Forest & the Hodder Valley by Greenwood & Bolton
Blackburn Tram Rides by Jim Halsall
A Blackburn Mixture by Bob Dobson

A full list of publication is available on request.

Contents

INTRODUCTION

My earliest recollection (I'm an Accrington lad) is of being on the railway station as a train spotter in the 1950's, followed by visits when a young policeman in the 1960's, to the Quarter Sessions and the County Record Office. Retirement from the Lancashire Constabulary turned me into a publisher and I published two books by Stephen Sartin - *"Preston a Century Ago"* and *"Preston Past and Present"*. My knowledge of, and fascination with, Lancashire's capital, gradually increased and I started to collect material which I might use at some time in a book. I had already compiled and published *"Mixture"* books on Blackpool, Blackburn and Accrington. The success of Stephen Sartin's *"Preston in Focus"* which I published in 2002, spurred me into the work needed to put together a collection of pieces of prose, poetry and photographs, all having something to do with Preston's past. I sought, and have received, contributions from local historians. I have spent many hours in my own research and have thoroughly enjoyed compiling this book. I hope Prestonians find it pleasurable.

My thanks are due to those contributors and the staff in the Harris Reference and Local Studies Library. I have thoroughly enjoyed liaising with these writers and librarians and am minded that I may follow my work up with another *"Preston Mixture"*. There is an enormous amount of interesting information on Preston's past to be preserved in prose. Lastly, I thank Stephen Sartin for the enthusiasm which fired me up to undertake this book and for his unfailing responses to my requests for his time and knowledge.

Bob Dobson

Bob Dobson

PRESTON FROM ABOVE

On Monday October 20th 1902, the first airship to be seen in the skies above Preston was spotted. Mr Stanley Spencer had set off from Blackpool and followed the Ribble over Preston before heading for a landing at Ulnes Walton. A person, possibly the editor Anthony Hewitson, was commissioned by the *'Preston Guardian'* to track him down. This he did by hiring a hansom cab. After greeting the intrepid aviator and talking over a cup of tea, he wrote *"Soon Preston came into view like a map with the street lines clear and the traffic like the movement of ants"*. The airship was constructed of bamboo and filled with hydrogen. This illustration was published in a Blackpool newspaper of the time.

TRUTH IS STRANGER.....

An item of news in *"The Gentleman's magazine"* of September 1736 takes some believing... *"On the 26th past, a man passing over the bridge over the Savoc(sic) near Preston, Lancashire, saw two large flights of birds meet with such rapidity that 180 of them fell to the ground, were taken up by him and sold in Preston Market that same day"*.

T'TRAMS

By Bob Dobson

Apart from the very early (1803) horse-drawn tramway which connected two stretches of the Lancaster Canal over the Ribble, the first tramway on Preston's streets was operated by *Preston Tramways Company* from 1879. It too was horse-drawn with two miles of 3ft 6ins gauge track between Lancaster Road and near Fulwood Barracks.

In 1882, William Harding, who already ran horse-buses in the town, leased a new system from the Corporation, who had invested in a modern, though still horse-drawn, infra structure. This involved two routes. The first ran from the Pleasure Gardens in New Hall Lane, through town to the river at what is now Penwortham Bridge. The other ran from the Town Hall through Tulketh to Ashton for two miles. Eight double-decked tramcars were sufficient for the service. Harding's lease expired in December 1903 and the Corporation took over the running from a new depot they had built off Lancaster Road.

The Corporation had seen that horse-power could be replaced by electricity. Two (1900 & 1902) Acts of Parliament had enabled it to expand the system in a big way – over eleven miles, over half of which was double-tracked – using electricity. The new tracks were of 4ft 8ins gauge and a new tram shed generating station was built in Deepdale to cater for the high-tech, 30-strong fleet, in their maroon and ivory livery. The generator and most engineering were supplied by *Dick, Kerr & Co* of Strand Road, a name which would become synonymous with that of Preston throughout the world. The 30 tramcars were built in Preston by the *Electric Railway & Tramcar Carriage Works Company.*

7th June 1903 was *"opening day"* for the first of two new routes – to the Barracks and to Farringdon Park. Later in the month *"cars"* would run out to Deepdale and Penwortham. Ashtoners had to wait until the following January because of a cost- saving decision by the Tramways Committee which brought widespread disapproval within the Council and the town.

A route down London Road to Walton was considered, bolstered by Walton-le-Dale UDC's pressuring. However, it never materialised. Similarly, plans to go West to Lytham and meet to link up with Blackburn and the rest of North East Lancashire never got off the ground.

The volume of people efficiently carried to their work and pleasure was enormous. However, the Corporation managed to build extra capacity into the strictly-adhered-to-timetables that allowed for *"specials"* to run within the town centre for shoppers and for supporters going to watch *"t'North End"*.

Over the years, the system was altered slightly, the number of cars increased and their design modernised – in some cases by simply covering over the top deck. One major milestone was the introduction of female conductors during the First World War, when the timetable was squeezed in the interests of economy. I imagine that not a few conductresses got squeezed too.

Although there were other tramcar makers in the country, all of Preston's cars were made by *Dick, Kerr's* and their successors the *United Electric Car Co.* and *English Electric.*

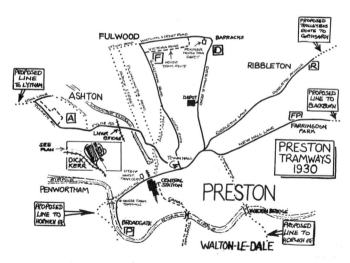

The plan shows certain letters which were used to identify the routes:
A = Ashton, D = Inner Circle, F = Outer Circle, FP = Farringdon Park,
P = Penwortham, R = Ribbleton, O = Other Workings.

The 1930's witnessed the beginning of the end for Preston's trams. Farringdon Park and Penwortham passengers lost their trams in favour of buses in 1932, the year in which the *Tramways Committee* became the *Transport Committee*. Ribbleton route soon followed, then Ashton. 15th December witnessed, without any celebration or tears, the last trams on the Fulwood and Deepdale lines. Twenty four tramcars became surplus, to be sold to other Local Authorities still persevering. The electric system had operated for thirty one years, carrying an estimated 370 million passengers over 32 million miles.

I am grateful to Peter Hesketh, author of *"Trams in the North West"* (1995 Ian Allan) for advice and the use of his map. I recommend his book to anyone seeking to know more about Lancashire's trams.

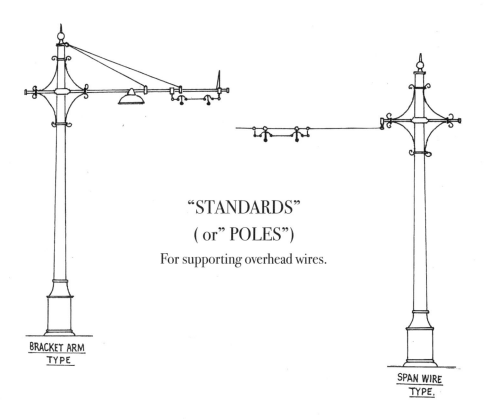

"STANDARDS"
(or" POLES")
For supporting overhead wires.

BRACKET ARM
TYPE

SPAN WIRE
TYPE.

THE PRESTON LAMB

I love to see the Preston Lamb,
It always makes me glad
Because it brings warm memories
About our special Dad.

When he had reached eleven years,
To his unbounded joy
He got a job – his very first,
He was a Parcel Boy
For Preston Corporation.
He rode on every tram,
He wore his uniform with pride –
And on his cap, the Lamb.

The Corporation Transport
He made his life's career
A little break to fight the War
Did nought to interfere.
As years went by the buses came
Replacing tram and line;
So Dad now drove the buses
We thought it very fine!

Each button on his overcoat;
And tunic that he wore,
A picture of the Preston Lamb
Most shinily they bore.
And then at school, to my delight
in uniform of blue,
On beret, panama, velour
I got to wear it too!

Tom Finney wore it on his shirt,
The Mayors on golden chain,
But every time I see the Lamb,
I see our Dad again.
Although I'm no-one special,
How very proud I am,
To have the honour and the right
To wear the Preston Lamb.

(Linda M Hughes)

Linda Hughes wrote this poem in memory of her dad, Jim Riley. He had started work for the Corporation in 1919 as a parcel boy, travelling on the trams. He progressed to 'bus conductor, driver and inspector, always wearing the Preston Lamb on his silver buttoned uniform. The parcel rates are for those in force when young Jim started on the trams. Doesn't he look fine?

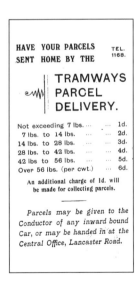

UNDERNEATH THE ARCHES - 1882

ARCH IN FISHERGATE.

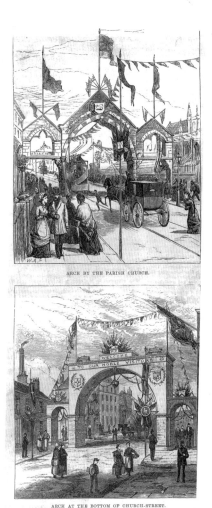

ARCH BY THE PARISH CHURCH.

ARCH IN PITT-STREET.

ARCH AT THE BOTTOM OF CHURCH-STREET.

How the Illustrated London News artist captured the 1882 Guild.

In June 1900 the *"English Electric Manufacturing Company"* opened a new factory on an 11-acre site in Strand Road. Opposite that of the *"Electric Tramways and Waggon Company"*. The new buildings were *"the finest set of their kind in the kingdom"*. The main workshop was practically a quarter of a mile long and 120 feet wide, equipped with two cranes. Through a succession of company names and ownership, including that of the far-famed *"Dick, Kerr and Company"* the buildings were acquired in 1918 by the newly-formed *"English Electric Company"* whose association with Preston was to remain until it became part of *"British Aerospace"*. The site was abandoned and sold for housing in the 1990's. These two photos show the interior of the Strand Road works in the late 1940's, when female labour introduced in the war years, was utilised on the shop floor.

HERE IS . . . .

THE NEW **BOND** RANGER

at £295

(IN PRIMER)

**HIRE PURCHASE
TERMS £59
INITIAL PAYMENT**

24 payments
of £11 . 8 . 2
per month

THE NEW **BOND** RANGER OPENS UP POSSIBILITIES OF
ECONOMICAL COMMERCIAL TRANSPORT AT A MODEST COST

★ Capacity : 31 cubic feet
★ Annual Tax £5 plus low Insurance rates

★ Colours: British Racing Green, Light Green
★ and Scarlet with Ivory hard top at only £4.10.0 extra

This 1960 advert tells the potential customer all he wants to know, concentrating on the # s d. Sharp's saved on advertising expense by using a local girl; probably out of their office, to give the advert some glamour.

This 1950 MK A is now in the care of the Museum of Lancashie and is *"As good as new"*.   (Photo - "The Museum of Lancashire").

14

THE BOND MINICAR
Nick Wotherspoon

The story of Preston's famous *"Bond Minicars"*, begins at Lawrence "Lawrie" Bond's workshop at Longridge, the prototype vehicle being constructed on the first floor of a former fire station and lowered through a trap-door to the workshop below. Putting the Minicar into production on these premises was not a serious option! Lawrie Bond realised this, hoped to lease space in Preston and made contact with Lt.-Col. Gray, director of Sharp's Commercials who had spare factory space in the town. The prototype for Lawrie's far-sighted *"shopping car"* concept had been announced in May 1948 and had led to considerable interest,no doubt due to the economic conditions at that time. The tiny vehicle utilised an all-aluminium semi-monocoque bodyshell and was powered by a 122cc Villiers motorcycle engine, mounted on a centrally positioned single front steering fork attached to the front bulkhead. It was a crude vehicle, with no rear suspension save for the cushioning effect of the 8" low pressure tyres and somewhat less than reliable *"cable & bobbin"* steering arrangement. However with a claimed fuel consumption of 104 mpg and a top speed of 30 mph it was not long before Lawrie began to receive serious inquiries with regard to sales and Col. Gray realised that with a little more development, here was a winner. A deal was struck and with Lawrie employed as a consultant, Sharp's began to plan for production, resulting in the announcement in November 1948 of a substantially different vehicle - the *"Bond Minicar"*.

The vehicle was launched with a publicity campaign featuring a series of endurance runs, which established an independently recorded fuel consumption figure of almost 100 mpg. *"Full"* production commenced in early 1949 at Sharp's Ribbleton Lane premises. Initially only some 15 vehicles a week were built - somewhat less than the 50 a week figure quoted by the company at the launch. But Sharp's were convinced that the little vehicles had potential and acquired the design and manufacturing rights. This gave them a free-hand to develop the concept, though the considerably remodelled production version of the Minicar still adhered to the construction concept of Lawrie's prototype. It took the form of an open two-seat tourer with limited luggage space behind the seats. There were no doors, in order to retain the shell's rigidity, but simply a slight curved cut-out to the cockpit side. This made entry and exit something of a feat when the hood was raised! Power was still provided by the 122cc engine, with improved steering and suspension. Sharp's Commercials Ltd also retained the Bond name for their vehicle, which although this no doubt made good sense from a marketing point of view, it was to lead to much confusion over the years - the company finally changing its name to *Bond Cars Ltd* as late as 1964!

As the Minicar gained popularity, the demand for a more practical and rugged vehicle led to the introduction of the *Mk B* model in July 1951. This similar looking vehicle featured a more powerful 197cc engine, as well as a number of features which had only been optional on the Mk A, such as a Triplex safety-glass windscreen in place of the previous model's easily damaged Perspex item and a re-designed hood. Initially only one model was offered, but in 1952 Sharp's introduced two new versions, initially attempting to branch out into the commercial market, by introducing the concept of the *"ultra-light"* commercial vehicle. The first of these was the *"Minitruck"*, which was almost identical externally to the standard Minicar, apart from a modified hood with a rear *"loading"* flap. Inside however, only a driver's seat fitted and a flat load platform extended from the rear over the normal passenger seat location. The second model was the *"Minivan"*, with an aluminium box, with a rear access door built in place of the rear of the Minicar body and a short hood to cover the gap between this and the windscreen frame. This was soon followed by a version with side windows and sideways-facing hammock style seats to accommodate two children in the rear and grandly titled the *"Family Safety Saloon"*. Apparently the *"Safety"* part referred to the fact that the rear door could only be opened from the outside!

The unveiling of Reliant's new *"Regal"* four-seat three-wheeler for 1952 saw the company waste no time in developing a new Minicar. A streamlined prototype Bond exhibited at the same 1951 show had attracted considerable interest and Sharp's Commercials set about developing this into a new production model - the *Mk C* which was announced in September 1952 with production commencing in January 1953. The new vehicle was quite different in appearance, though Lawrie Bond's monocoque body-tub still formed its basis. It had large dummy front wings, which were not merely decorative, but allowed room for a completely new steering mechanism to be utilised. This allowed the front wheel drive unit to turn 180° lock to lock and gave the Mk C the ability to be turned around within it's own diagonal length. This was to become something of a trademark of the Bond Minicar. With a confirmed fuel consumption of 85-90 mpg, Sharp's advertising heralded it as "The world's most economical car" and initially 3 models were offered; a three seat *"Standard"* model, a *"De-Luxe"* model with electric starting and the *"Minitruck"* light commercial version. These were soon joined by a *"Family Safety"*, fitted with two rear sideways facing hammock style seats for children using the slightly extended bodyshell and utilising the hood already used for the Minitruck. The Mk C continued in production until 1956 with some 6,700 leaving the Preston factory and was followed by the almost identical in appearance *Mk D* Minicar.

World events favoured Sharp's - the *Suez Crisis* loomed heavily in the news and economy again became the order of the day. Though the re-styled front grill and rear wings readily identify the Mk D models, most of the changes were in the form of mechanical improvements, including the adoption of the SIBA Dynastart unit - which was available with a reversing option. The latter allowed the engine to be started in either direction - giving Minicars an effective reverse gear - ALL the gears in reverse. Sharp's had discovered that many of their customers were former motorcyclists who now had families. As the Minicar could be driven on a motorcycle licence this became a major selling point. In fact the Mk D proved to be the company's most popular model to date, so much so that the proposed introduction of a new model in December of 1956 was shelved. Sales were healthy enough that the cost of re-tooling for the new model could be deferred whilst the current model's popularity was exploited.

Production of the new *Mk E* Minicarcommenced in January 1958, with a completely redesigned aluminium body using a box section steel *"chassis"* riveted to the underside. This gave sufficient rigidity to allow the incorporation of full size doors and allowed for the design of a more streamlined and conventional looking vehicle. However there was a considerable weight penalty to this new design, which led to it being under-powered. As the Mk E was intended to complement the existing Mk D range, which remained in production, and also no doubt influenced by its poor performance, it was only offered as a three-seater *"Tourer"* model. The interior was spacious compared to previous models and the bench front seat could accommodate three adults. Though the Mk E was by far the most practical and conventional looking of the Minicars so far, initial teething problems and the poor performance meant that it never really took off and in November 1958 the model was discontinued, with only 1,800 built.

In late 1958 Sharp's decided to completely update the range and announced three new models based on the modern appearance of the new bodyshell: a three-seat *Tourer,* a four-seat *Family Saloon* and a three-seat *Saloon/Coupé.* Due to demand, the Mk D Family Saloon remained in production unchanged. The new *Mk F* models were fitted with 246cc Villiers engine, giving a respectable 55 mph top speed. The new range was an immediate success, with production at Sharp's reaching almost 100 Minicars per week by April 1959. Such was the Minicar,s popularity, the company published a quarterly journal - *The Bond Magazine.* It contained news of developments to the current models and of modifications available to update and improve older vehicles. Also included were tips for home service and repair , as well as adverts for a wide range of accessories available for Minicars. It also contained news from the network of Bond Minicar Owners Clubs which had grown up throughout the country. Although the Mk F proved to be the company's most popular Minicar with some 7000 being built, Sharp's could hardly rest on their laurels. The 1950s were coming to a close and the 1959 Motorshow was to be one of the most important since the war. Although economy was still a consideration, the restrictions and crisis that had given the Minicar such a boost were now giving way to fashion. The show saw many totally new vehicles, including the *Ford Anglia, Triumph Herald* and most important of all - *The Mini.*

Sharp's answered by updating the Minicar yet again in September of 1961, with the *Mk G* range. Despite its similar appearance to the previous model, the company was taking the competition seriously and the Mk G featured many improvements. The engine was updated to the new Villiers 246cc Mk35A engine, the rear suspension was redesigned and incorporated trailing arms, coil springs and hydraulic shock absorbers.The brakes were brought up to date with a Lockheed hydraulic system. The passenger compartment was redesigned to give more room and on the Saloon models a cut-back rear window was incorporated to improve the headroom over the rear seats, which now could accommodate two adults in comfort. Other refinements included: opening quarter lights, wind-up door windows, improved interior trim and 10" wheels - all intended to give the Minicar a more conventional *"real"* car feel! Initially only the four-seat *250G* model was offered, but in 1962 an *Estate* model was added to the range featuring a large, top-hinged tail-gate, giving excellent access and a fold-down rear seat to give the options of load or passenger carrying capacity. Despite the competition, the Minicar seemed to be holding its own - road tax for three-wheelers and a lower rate of purchase tax for such vehicles no doubt helped. The 250G Estate was very well received and even achieved the distinction of being one of the very few three-wheelers to be the subject of a full *Autocar* Road test. However 1962 was not to be a good year for Sharp's, with the lowering of purchase tax on conventional vehicles, but without any concession for three-wheelers, this removed one of the major attractions. Furthermore the Motorcycle Show in November of that year saw the launch by Reliant of their new *Regal* - now powered by an alloy 598cc overhead-valve engine of their own design and remarkably competitively priced. Sharp's responded by offering a new engine option for the Minicar using the 249cc Villiers Mk4T twin cylinder engine giving increased power and performance, but it made little difference. The Mk G soldiered on, but efforts to promote the range failed to revive flagging sales. Production continued as late as 1966, but only to order and with a total of just over 3000 Mk G vehicles being built, it ceased. After 15 years production and some 26,500 Minicars rolling off the production line, the story as far as the Minicar was concerned came to an end.

UP, UP AND AWAY

Bob Dobson

The invention and production of coal-gas resulted in inflation – of air balloons for air travel. Possibly the first flight over Preston – not the first in Lancashire – took place during the Guild celebrations in September 1822 when a Mr Livingstone *"rose majestically"* before ten thousand gawping Guilders. The intrepid explorer's craft lost height near Whalley, its grappling iron causing damage to everything it came into contact with, including a tree which it uprooted. Livingstone fell 18ft onto a field, bruising himself considerably. His balloon crashed near Selby.

In 1825, George Green, a member of a family boasting several balloonists, made two flights from Preston. On one of them he travelled to Settle (28 miles) at 79 mph. A few years later he flew from Preston and was landing near the canal at Blackburn when a young lad caught hold of the craft's grappling iron, intending to anchor it. Still holding the rope, he was carried upwards for a short distance.

Green returned to Preston yet again in August 1849. In the 60ft high *"Rainbow"* balloon, he made the first ascent from Preston for 21 years, watched by a huge crowd clinging to lamp-posts and church steeples. Some men on the roof of the Corn Exchange found themselves imperilled when the balloon struck the weather vane and was torn. The observers *"were in no small peril of having their craniums damaged"*. Green landed safely and returned to the town later in the month, then flying to Accrington to be *"greeted by and enormous and excited crowd"*.

Here's the staff of Carter's Stanley Garage and Motor Works in New Hall Lane at the corner of Stanley Street in 1908. My suspicion is that Arthur Winter, one of the town's foremost professional photographers has "touched up" the firm's name and at least one of the car registration plates. The firm advertised that they were *"open day and night"*, and were agents for Englebert's oils. They also taught the new skill of driving motor cars - give them a ring on 80 Y 5.

This photo was probably taken about 1892 for the Corporation or the Ribble Navigation Company. With a man on top of the iron gates and another seen through the gap at the bottom, it gives an impression of the enormity and power of these titanic tide-holders.

Edwardian Prestonians liked taking their refreshment in style. Here we see (upper Photo) inside Mr Cookson;s *"White Horse"* Restaurant, opposite the Post Office in Friargate. It was large enough to accommodate funeral parties and the like and had adjacent meeting rooms for social gatherings. The *"Ribblesdale"* (lower photo) was not so grandly named or equipped, but did a good trade in luncheons and afternoon teas. *"Ribblesdale Iced Cake"* went down well with tea and coffee. The fire provided a homely, welcoming touch seldom fond in today's caffs, bistros or diners.

OLD PRESTON DOCK'S NEW DAY

No more they sail to briny seas,
On Ribble's rolling tide,
Those merchant ships, if now you please,
To other ports they glide.

Once harbour gates swung open wide,
Came wood and pulp and clay,
And outward cargoes, none denied,
Now all have gone for aye!

O Albert Edward Dock take heart,
You've finer role to play;
Though wounded sore, and torn apart,
There dawns a brighter day!

Those little yachts with time to spare,
Will breeze on pleasure bent;
And folks enjoy marina there,
That part to leisure lent.

New industries will rise and use
Those hectares tucked away;
Delightful dwellings with rich views,
Will grace the Ribble's way!

Excitingly, despair has ceased,
"Old Salt" has sailed away!
His sun has set. Salute, turn East,
Now dawns the dock's new day!

Christopher Reddington Shaw (1983)

THE FIRST TAXI?

Preston's connection with the hansom cab is well known – Joseph Aloysius Hansom designed St. Walburge's church as well as the horse-drawn carriage which bears his name (1834), but when did Preston's association with such, or similar carriages, start? The answer is contained in a letter from Mr Robert Clarke which was published in the *'Preston Guardian'* on 24th August 1869.

THE FIRST CAB IN PRESTON

I have in my possession an original card announcing the first cab (or, as they were then styled, "Bath Carriage") in Preston. It reads as follows:-"Bath Carriage. – J. Croft respectfully informs the Ladies and Gentlemen of Preston that he has intro- duced into this Town, one of those fashionable vehicles, a Bath Carriage, and begs to solicit the patronage of the public. The Carriage may be had at a Moment's Notice by applying at the Legs of Man, opposite the Town Hall, on the following terms:- One Person conveyed to any part of the town within the Bars 1s., and back again before midnight, 6d.: or 1s. after midnight. Two persons the same distance 2s., and back again 1s. before midnight, or 2s. after. If engaged by the hours, 2s. per hour – N.B. Post Chaise and Carriages as usual. Preston, November 27th, 1821. – I. Wilcockson, Printer, Preston." – The Mr J. Croft above mentioned was the father of the late Mr. Edward Croft, who was at the Victoria Hotel so many years.

ANOTHER FIRST IN TRANSPORT

A *"sedan chair"* is a device in which one person is carried in a compartment, usually by two men. It was popular in the 17th and 18th centuries. It is believed that the first one seen in Preston was introduced during the 1822 Guild by Mr R Langton, one of the town's bailiffs.

* * * * * * * *

In May 1868, Thomas Hilton died. Who was he and what was his claim to fame? He was the first porter employed at Preston Railway Station when it was opened by the North Union Railway in 1838, and proudly wore a brass number "**1**" on his arm. He was 66 years old when he died, still a porter after thirty years.

AFLOAT IN THE RIBBLE

Bob Dobson

The story of Preston's connections with its river, the docks, with ships and with trading with the world is a long, interesting one. The town, in the form of the Corporation, has always played a part alongside *"the private sector"* and an example of that co-operation came to public notice on Saturday 25th February 1865, at 11.20am to be precise.

At that time, the townsfolk were still feeling the effect of *"the Cotton Famine"*, which had so badly hit Preston's major industry – cotton weaving and spinning.

The event was the launching of the first vessel made by the newly formed *"Preston Iron Ship Building Company"*. The *"Ada Wilson"* was a screw-driven steamer, a 2-masted schooner, 226 feet long overall, 28 feet across the beam, and weighed 500 tons. She was fitted with accommodation for forty first-class passengers – and of course was *"A.a. at Lloyd's"*. She had been built by the company in their yard on the Marsh end (which was probably leased from the Corporation for a period of several years) for their own use in order to act as a showpiece and give a stimulus to other companies who might wish to carry goods from Preston to the world, and back again.

The launch was a first-class affair befitting a Preston *"first"*. The Mayor and several members of the Corporation were present to see the wife of Mr Wilson, the company's chairman *"christen"* her. Unfortunately the tide was four feet higher than anticipated, with the result that the vessel *"dipped"* into the river *"in capital style"*, sailed rapidly across and bumped her rudder into the far bank. No damage was caused and she was said to be *"sound as a bottle"*. The mishap, in which a restraining chain was broken, was put down to the incorrect angle of the slipway. However, the vessel was turned around, towed to the quayside and tied up to await her journey to Liverpool to be *"fitted out"*.

What then? A celebratory luncheon at the *"Red Lion"* for about a hundred invited guests. Mr Wilson *"took the chair"*, so it appears that the company paid for the meal and accompanying wines, as well as for the services of the Preston Rifle Corps band.

After the meal – toasts and speeches. Mr Wilson proposed *"health"* to the Queen, the rest of the Royal family, to the Army, the Navy and the Volunteers.

Next on his feet was Mr Moss, who was the only other member of the Preston Iron Ship Building Company, along with Mr Wilson. They employed a Mr Smith as chief engineer and workmen in their yard. Both were Liverpool men who had had the f oresight to see that Liverpool was fully developed as a port and ship building centre, and that Preston had enormous potential.

First of all, he apologised for the fact that the Town Clerk, Mr Ascroft hadn't been invited. (It would be difficult to think of a bigger *"clanger"* to drop, for his company was going to need all the co-operation it could get from the Corporation and the Town Clerk was the man who would give the OK on any liaison. That was potentially a far greater mistake than positioning a slipway at too acute any angle. (It isn't what you know - it's who you know).

He went on to talk of his company's vision for seeing the river crowded with docks, with ships coming and going, for *"the Ribble is far better than the Clyde for navigation"* (Applause). He anticipated that the population of Preston would *"double itself in thirty years if docks were laid down"*. Another vessel was under construction and the company had orders for two more. The company had started off building *"on our own account ..... to show what could be done in Preston (Applause)- If there were dry docks in Preston, the trade would be enormously extended"*. He appeared to hint that if the Corporation had built dry docks, using the available manpower during the recent long period of unemployment, they would have *"wanted very little relief from the funds for distressed operatives – they would all have found work in shipbuilding or the adjuncts thereof in Preston"*.

The Mayor thanked Mr Moss for the nature of his toast. He agreed that Preston, with the Ribble and plenty of land alongside, had a great potential for river-related trade and industry, comparing it to the Clyde. All that was wanted was *"a little bit more enterprise on the part of the wealthy inhabitants to make it what it ought to have been".* (Applause) (Was he shifting responsibility away from the Corporation which Mr Moss had criticised?).

He hoped that future leaders would be as successful as today's, and wished the *"Ada Wilson"* a career as successful as the launch. He believed there would be no backwardness on the Corporation's part in future discussions.

Alderman Spencer, a director of the *'Ribble Navigation Company'* then wished success to the shipbuilding venture and echoed the sentiments expressed by Mr Moss – he had thought so for many years. *"The Corporation of Preston do not give the Ribble the countenance which they ought to have done. This ought not to be the case ......* " He went on further, holding little back in criticising the Corporation's track record, to applause and shouts of *"Hear, Hear".* He knew that the Corporation had spent money in providing quayside facilities, *"but forgot to say that the sum has not been sufficient to the requirements of the case".* He urged them to think on a grander scale alongside the board of the Ribble Navigation Company. He promised his support for the host company.

Alderman Parker, also a director of the Ribble Navigation Company wasn't so barbed. He recalled that in his 18 years on the company's board there had been many ups and downs. Bankruptcy hadn't been very far away at one time. All that was needed was cordial co-operation between the company and the Corporation to *"to realise success".* The first object was *"more water".* He wished success to the new venture.

The Mayor responded without taking arms. The day had seen the launching of the biggest Preston-built ship to date and success to both the Preston Iron Ship Company and the borough.

A few further toasts were drunk and thanks expressed before *"the room was subsequently cleared and a dancing party was formed. The gyrations of the company were kept up to the strains of the rifle band for a considerable time, and all enjoyed themselves most heartily".*

That excellent book *"The Last Tide : a History of the Port of Preston 1806-1981 "* by Jack Dakres casts doubt upon the claim that this was the biggest ship so far built in

Preston. I also recommend
"The History of the Ribble Navigation from Preston to the Sea" by James Barron
(1938).

A 1950's postcard view of Preston Docks

A TALE OF THREE PLAQUES.
Terry Regan

The following names were taken entirely at random, from a list of almost two thousand such names, which are carved into the huge and imposing stone memorial tablets situated on the walls adjacent to the main staircases` of The Harris Museum in Preston.

The people named on these stones are all casualties of the First World War. They are all Preston men who, in the flower of their youth, had their lives snatched from them in the most horrendous fashion, during that bloodiest of obscene conflicts.

Although the stone memorials at the Harris give only scant detail with regard to these poor souls, and others, there is an almost definitive list known as *"Preston's Roll Of Honour"*, which is deposited in the Reference Library in the same building. This gives a lot of detail concerning the majority of those local men who fell during the *"war to end all wars"*

At this point, I sincerely apologise to any person who might be related to any of those names chosen at random, and who might feel aggrieved at this inclusion.

John Joseph Adams
19, Walton Street, Preston. Occupation; Labourer; 2nd Battalion, Loyal North Lancs. Rank, Private, Number 10211. Date of death, 25th, March. 1915.Killed, German East Africa.

*   *   *   *

Christopher Ainsworth
217 Fletcher Road, Preston. Occupation; Carter; Number 1 section, 271 Machine Gun corps. Rank, Private, Number 99786. Date of death, May 27th, 1918. Killed on the sea; torpedoed.

*   *   *   *

John Boothby
22 Curwen Street, Preston. Occupation; Plasterer; Northumberland Fusiliers. Rank not given. Date of death, not given. Remarks; Missing since June 5th 1917. Never heard of since.

Henry Seed

23 Springfield Street, Preston. Occupation; Plumber. Royal Engineers. Rank,
Sapper, Number, 498576. Date of death;
September 28th,, 1918. Killed; Cambria, France.

* * * *

James Seddon

58 Ashmoor Street, Preston. Occupation; Book keeper. East Lancashire
Regiment. Rank; Private, Number 31003.
Date of death; October 10th, 1918.
Died a prisoner of war in Germany.

* * * *

George Frederick Glaister

22 St Pauls Square, Preston. Occupation;
Master of the Kings School, Chester.
Royal Tank Corps. Number not given. Date of death;
August 1st, 1918. Killed, between Albert and Armentiers.

* * * *

Harold Ernest Livesey

387 St Georges Road, Preston. Occupation; Organ Builder. Highland Light
Infantry. Rank, Lance Corporal, Number 32626. Date of death; July 10th,
1917.
Killed; Near Neuforts, but not sure, no grave.

* * * *

Richard Howarth

13 Barlow Street, Preston. Occupation; Cotton Spinner. 10th Service
Battalion, Loyal North Lancs. Rank, Lance Corporal, Number 12636.
Date of death; January 25th, 1917.
Drowned when crossing a moat in the Somme.

* * * *

Robert Taylor

68 Euston Street, Preston. Occupation; Crane Driver.
Lancashire Fusiliers. Rank, Private, Number 205101.
Date of Death; Presumed killed by War Office, September 20th, 1917.
Killed at Ypres.

James Lamb
2 Wren Street, Preston. Occupation; Insurance Clerk.
2nd Royal Inniskilling Fusiliers. Rank; Private, Number 49465. Date of
death; April 29th, 1918. Killed, near Ypres.
Remarks; Left for France on Easter Sunday, March 31st, 1918.

* * * *

And Finally.
Sydney Reynolds
211 Shelley Street, Preston. Occupation; Railway stoker.
1st Battalion Loyal North Lancs. Rank; Private, Number 20116. Date of
death; December 30th, 1917.
Killed; drowned troop ship Aragon in the Eastern Med. Received wounds twice
previously in France, on the Somme, and at Messines Ridge.

Quite apart from the obvious fact that all of the above named were casualties of the First World War, and all came from Preston, there are several other remarkable facts worth mentioning., which tie these proud men closer than ever. During the First World War, Preston was a major embarkation point for many of the British and Allied troops who, were going off to the various battle fronts, throughout Europe, Africa, and the Middle East.

The majority of these troops who departed from the town went by train, and it is almost certain that if not all, then at least the largest majority of the above named men, and those whose names can be found in the Harris Museum, left their native town by train from its railway station. I cannot give a written guarantee that these men did catch a train from Preston, but it seems highly likely that they did in fact embark via train from this station on their way to war. The railway was by far the largest mass rapid transport movement during those troubled times. The following will lend weight to my suggestions.

On Preston railway station, there are three simple bronze plaques situated on the walls of the waiting room which adjoins both platforms three, and four. To my mind these plaques strongly suggest that the above named soldiers would have embarked from these very platforms. But how can one be sure? You may well ask this pertinent question; the answer lies for the whole world to see, simply in the thought provoking text that is depicted on the largest of the three plaques, which reads as follows.

During the Great War of 1914-1919, this room was by the permission of The L & NW and L & Y Railway Companies, occupied from August 19th 1915 to November 11th 1919, by the Preston Station Sailors and Soldiers Free Buffet Association of Voluntary Workers who, supplied the Three and Three quarter millions of the Soldiers and Sailors who passed through this station, with refreshments and comforts.

The room from August 19th, 1915 to May 31st, 1919 was open continuously day and night, and from June 1st 1919 to November 11th 1919 for fourteen hours each day.

Two smaller plaques, which until quite recently were attached to stone plinths on platforms three and four, show a rather condensed version of events. Now having been restored to their former glory by the Museum of Lancashire in Stanley street, working under the directions of Virgin Trains, they too have been emplaced in the waiting room ,on the wall opposite the largest of the trio.

Three and Three Quarter Millions!

So; here we have it, Three and three quarter million men passed through this station on their way to war. That figure is quite staggering, for it represents over one third of the force which Britain and its Empires unleashed against the Hun! Perhaps, as many as two thousand of these men hailed from Preston. An extremely large number from one town alone. The town was robbed of the cream of its youth, every fallen son's life was precious, every family so afflicted by these horrible events grieved just as badly as those in other places, which included almost every town, city and village in Great Britain, and many throughout the Empire.

These men came from many different regiments. Not just the obvious ones such as the *Loyal North Lancs,* and the *East Lancs,* etc, and as the plaque states very clearly, also included members of the Royal Navy who, along with the troops were dispersed to many battle fronts. Some of these men were being sent

to almost certain death, though during the early stages of the war when there was no shortage of volunteers, it wouldn't have seemed that way, for wasn't this war going to be *"over by Christmas"*?
As the flood of volunteers trickled to a stream, conscription became necessary.

The obscene number of casualties, especially in France and Belgium had depleted our forces greatly, so that by now some young men were not quite so eager to put their lives on the line, despite the best efforts of the misguided *"White Feather Brigade"*.

The war was eventually won, but at what price? The cream of Europe's youth had been decimated, as had those of the Empire, and to a lesser degree America. Millions of those brave young, and not so young' men had passed through Preston railway station on the horrendous road to war, a one-way journey for some. Assuming a death rate of only ten per cent, which according to official figures is on the low side, we can safely say that approximately three hundred and seventy five thousand of those who did embark from Preston, were going on a one way ticket to Hell! That figure is roughly equal to the combined, present day populations of both Preston, and Blackpool. The total number of wounded was probably at least treble that figure, which would mean that of all the troops who left Preston by train during those few short years, well over a million would eventually be killed or wounded in action, and that figure almost equates with the population of the whole of the present county of Lancashire, and actually represents at least a third of all those fighting men who passed through those waiting rooms on Preston station. Some allowance has to be made for the possibility that some of the three and three quarter million soldiers mentioned on the plaques may actually have been returning home, but as there appear to be no definitive figures which might support this theory, one has to assume that the plaques refer to those on their way to the front.

Imagine those tumultuous scenes during those war years; the constant comings and goings night and day; in the waiting rooms welcome cups of tea and coffee were drunk by the million, sandwiches, pies and the like consumed by the shipload no doubt, and all provided by those guardian angels, the volunteers of Preston railway station waiting rooms. No doubt during the first few months of the war, there would have been jubilant laughter and bravado in and around those waiting rooms, but as the war ground on, and early casualty figures emerged, the mood changed. Can one possibly imagine how many tearful farewells took place on those platforms? Is it possible to imagine how frightened many of those young men and boys were, even though the majority wouldn't have shown it? How many wives, mothers and sweethearts, bid a heart- rending farewell to their lads?

How many fathers and brothers wept a silent tear as they bade "au revoir" to their beloved ones, and how many would weep openly on hearing the news that they would never see them again? Life would never be the same for anyone!

On no account must we ever be allowed to forget these fine men. They must not have died in vain.

"MISS PUNCH" – A PRINCESS OF THE PRESTON PLATFORM

The local papers carried an announcement in April 1890 of the death of a Mrs Emily Barclay, 50yrs, of Southport. She was interred in Preston Cemetery. The announcement escaped the attention of many, but not that of the editor of the *'Preston Herald'.* He told his readers that Emily was a lady who, forty years previously had been one of the pioneers of the railway bookstall system. During the hey-day of her career as a railway news- vendor and bookseller, her stall on Preston station was the fashionable lounge and local news exchange.

Miss Emily Lambert, more generally known as *"Miss Punch"*, was known by all who travelled the London to Scotland line, as well as locals. About 1850, whilst living with her mother who kept a small shop off Friar Gate, she conceived the idea that a stall on the platform, stocked with sundries would be profitable. She got permission. At first she sold sweets, cake and ginger beer, then started to stock magazines and weekly papers. This was before the availability of daily papers.Her turnover increased, due in no small way to her pleasant, impish way with customers.

In 1862, when the *'Cotton Famine'* brought poverty to Preston, Emily collected enough from her customers to pay for 7,460 people to be fed over five days, consuming an enormous amount of bread, tea and coffee.

Young Emily left her stall, where she almost certainly met such literary giants as Charles Dickens, on becoming the wife of a Scottish businessman and going to live at Southport.

These are fine examples of the use of Preston plumbers of pictorial invoice heading on which the firm displays their speciality. Printed in Preston.

Executors of the Late Wm. Yates　**PRESTON,** *Dec. 31st 1885*

To Westray & Woods, Dr.
(SUCCESSORS TO W. CROOK.)
PLUMBERS, GLAZIERS,
House, Sign & Ornamental Painters, Gilders,
PAPER HANGERS, &c.

ANCHOR COURT, MARKET PLACE,

1885

174, NEW HALL LANE, PRESTON,

Messrs. Thos. Hewitt & Son　　Branch Shop: CAMBRIDGE ROAD, LYTHAM.

July 30 19 07

To JOSEPH HESKETH, R.P.C., F.I.S.E. & SON,
(Registered by the Worshipful Company of Plumbers.)

HOUSE, SIGN,
AND ORNAMENTAL
PAINTERS.
PAPER HANGING

ELECTRIC
BELLS & LIGHTS
FIXED.
GLAZING

PLUMBERS　　**GAS FITTERS**

AND GENERAL DECORATORS

IMPROVED PENDULUM INDICATOR
HALL · PARLOUR · BED R

Pumps, Baths, Water Closets, &c., neatly fitted up and repaired.

Terms: Contracts Nett Cash.　General A/cs. due Monthly.　5 % on overdue accounts.

1901
Jan 16/1901　Worthington Estate　new Hot water tap fixed Fishwick Parade　| 5 | 3 |

44?

LAWSON · STREET · FOUNDRY,

PRESTON, *July* 188*7*

Messrs. Houghton Myers & Riveley

To CHARLES SEWARD
PATENTEE & MANUFACTURER OF
Hot Water Apparatus
Iron & Brass Founder, Gas Engineer & Bell Hanger,
STOVE, CRATE & KITCHEN RANGE MANUFACTURER.

TERMS
*Contracts Nett Cash.
Consolidation due Quarterly.
Interest charged on the ruled
5 per cent on overdue accounts*

1887

April 2　Repairing Boiler at Golden Hill

Chat to old Preston folk about the town before the Second World War and the talk will get around to memories of the *"Shrimp Women"* who brought their seafood fresh from Southport to the market to tempt Preston's palate. The accompanying photo was taken in the early years of the twentieth century, the poem was written by Rev. Alexander Reynolds, vicar of Winmarleigh and published in 1942. I have been unable to obtain copyright permission to use this poem, and do so in the hope that it will please his descendants to see his work remembered.

THE SHRIMP LADY.

The lady sits there all alone,
    Away from all the stalls ;
A wooden stool her royal throne,
    The skies her royal halls.

She sits aloof from all the flares
    Of shouting cheap-jacks there ;
She has no need to call her wares,
    She sells a goodly share.

Before her, on a table set,
  With cloth as white as snow,
There rises high the pinkest yet
  Of shrimps you ever saw.

The shrimps themselves attract your eye ;
  They look so fine and good ;
But best of all is that lady
  Upon her throne of wood.

Her frock is long and full and neat,
  Its stripes are white and blue ;
Starched cuffs and collars make complete
  A dress no longer new.

Her face, all rosy, wrinkled, clean,
  'Neath bonnet stiff and white,
Beams like the sun's most radiant gleam,
Dispelling shades of night.

Her eyes are gentle, good and wise,
  She looks so steadily
And kindly at the one who buys
  Her wares so readily.

Her voice is low and rather rough,
  She never went to school,
But it bespeaks her charm enough,
  As she sits on her stool.

" These shrimps, my dear, are sixpence for
  A half a gill, good measure.
It's nice to-day. You will have more ?
  To serve you is a pleasure."

Her age is long gone past the span
  Of three score years and ten,
But she can vie with any man
  In wit and acumen.

I see her every Saturday,
I look up for her smile,
I know exactly just the way
She'll look at me awhile.

If I have been away somewhere,
Returning, my first glimpse
Of pleasant things must be of her,
The lady who sells shrimps.

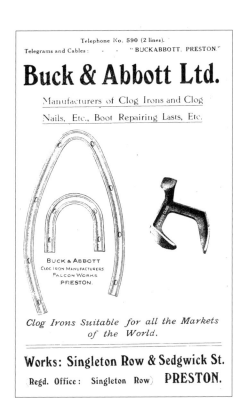

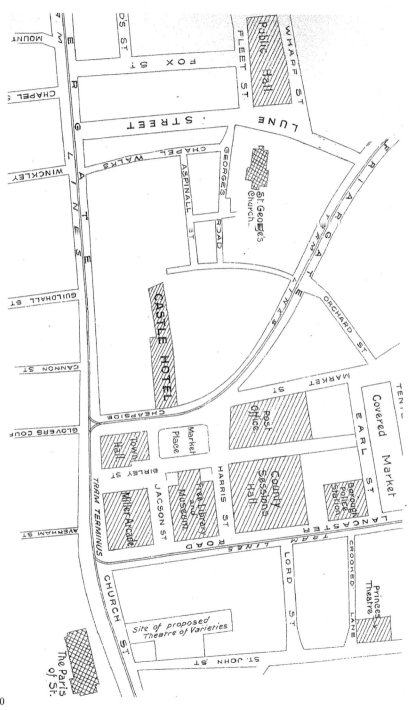

THE CASTLE INN
Marian Roberts.

Who, in Preston, has heard of the '*Castle Inn*'? It was built in the Market Place in 1623 and became a favourite coaching inn. Later it was named the '*Castle Hotel*' and was the meeting place of early Building Societies, including those of Fulwood and Ashton Freehold Parks, and Insurance Companies, as well as being a favourite hostelry where great events were celebrated, such as the rearing of the new Town Hall in 1865 when one hundred and fifty workmen were entertained to a substantial dinner at the joint expense of the Corporation and the contractors. Again, on the 29thDecember 1868 after the ceremonial opening of the Workhouse in Watling Street Road, Fulwood, '*the whole assembly of guests boarded their modes of transport to proceed to a dinner at the Castle Inn at 2pm.*'

About 1910 the Castle Hotel was purchased by the Refuge Assurance Company, transformed into commercial premises of a different nature, and named '*Castle Chambers*'. Their Preston office occupied rooms on the first floor whilst others in the building were leased to various tenants. It may surprise many of you to know that one of these tenants was the Football League, as stated in **Barrett's Trade Directory 1922. Football League (The) Ltd., Castle Chambers Market Place, Tel.304. Telegrams "League," Preston. T. Charnly, Secretary.**

I lived with my family at Castle Chambers from 1925 to 1949; we had a large flat there, and from the windows of the front office had a grandstand view of the great civic events which took place on the market square before the demolition of the town hall. We loved to see the Royal visits, the processions which accompanied successive mayors to church, the crowds that greeted the return of Preston North End, especially those of 1938 when the team won the F.A. Cup, the Whitsuntide Fair, the Pot Fair, and the projection on a giant screen of Election results. We saw, too, the burning of the Town Hall in March 1947, my own first view of this being from my bedroom at 1am., when I awoke just as the fingers of the clock fell to the ground.

In the days of my youth I spent almost every evening in the Harris Museum directly opposite to Castle Chambers, for in those days all departments remained open till a late hour, with very few people attending. I loved to see the stuffed birds, the birds' eggs in drawers in a cabinet, and the doll's house which stood in one of the galleries upstairs. Amongst the Beattie prints which lined the staircase wall was one of the

Castle Hotel, the caption of which told us that it was built in 1623 and that when it was converted to become Castle Chambers the original Jacobean staircase and some of the old beams were removed by Preston solicitor Mr. Arthur Theodore Ransome Houghton and placed in 'The Stone House', his home in Whittingham Lane, Broughton. Very many years later I was to see these features for myself, the beams built into the external wall of the 'Stone House', and the Jacobean staircase installed within.

Later still I was able to delve into the history of the 'Castle' and one of the first things I discovered was in the 'History of Preston' room at the Harris Museum where, displayed in a glass case was a piece of medieval pottery found in the Castle Inn Yard!

From Whittle's 'History of Preston' (1837) I discovered :
"The Castle Inn, in the Market Place was erected in 1623, and was at that time deemed an elegant building. A fine chimney piece was placed in a room over the gateway, consisting of a frontispiece (over the fireplace) carved with a mass of miniature columns, arches, niches and caryatids, piled up to the ceiling. The columns were after the grecian style (instead of gothic) supporting an incongruous body of arches after the Roman style of architecture. This piece of work was executed by Lawrence Winstanley, carver in Preston. Some time ago this was taken down by Col. Rawstorne of Penwortham, who no doubt will appreciate the value of it. The Castle Inn has been re-edified of late years."

From Vol. I, page 41 we learn that amongst minor news-rooms established in the town was that of '*the Royal Union, at the Castle Inn, Market-place*' and, on page 38 of the same volume the Market place itself is described as '*very spacious, consists of beautiful shops elegantly adorned with bey (sic) windows dressed out in the most fashionable manner by the respective tradespeople resident within its precincts – drapers, milliners, grocers, straw-hat makers, hatters, booksellers, brush-makers, shoe warehouses, hosiers, muslin and haberdashery warehouses, watch-makers, confectioners, china shops, braziers &c.'*

From *Oakey's Directory* of 1853 I learnt that coaches left the Castle Inn, Market Place to **Blackpool** *on Wednesday and Saturday*, **Burnley** *on Saturday*, **Kirkham,** *on Wednesday and Saturday*, **Padiham** *on Monday, Wednesday, and Saturday*, **Pilling** *on Saturday, and* **Whalley** *on Saturday.*

We now go further back to the Parliamentary Election of 1826 and the memorable visit to the Castle Inn of William 'Gridiron' Cobbett. This was recalled by Preston Historian, J.H. Spencer, in an article in the *Preston Herald* of 17th August 1945 which began: "*The election of 1826 was one of the most exciting of the remarkable contests of Preston. The polling occupied fifteen days; there were four candidates and each represented a different party, with its own committee, reports of meetings, broadsides and tracts, squibs, rhymes, appeals and notifications. I question whether in any previous or subsequent parliamentary election of the borough such a variety and quantity of printed matter was ever published. This was mostly due to William Cobbett the radical candidate who was a prince of pamphleteers, He had strong and forceful opinions about the treatment of the workers, and published trenchant satires and judgments upon public men...*"

When Cobbett reached Walton-le-dale on Whit Monday 1826 he was greeted by a wildly enthusiastic crowd who took the horses from the shafts of his carriage and, gathering green boughs, (green and white being the radical colours), drew it to Preston, "*proceeding throughout to the deafening shouts of the crowd. On men's shoulders he was carried into the Castle Inn, and from one of the windows, in a great speech, surpassed himself.*"

William Cobbett, Radical, did not win the election; the successful candidates were E.G. Stanley, (Whig), and John Wood, (Liberal). This had been an inflammatory contest with suspicions of trickery in the voting as practised in the Corn Exchange, Lune Street. On the evening after the declaration of the poll, Cobbett addressed his supporters before leaving the town; he said, "*Whether absent or present, distant or near, the people of Preston will till the last moment of my life, always be amongst the objects dear to my heart*".

I have been thrilled to receive, from the Harris Reference Library, a photo-copy of an old plan of the Castle Inn showing accommodation &c. It includes a map of the centre of Preston showing the exact position of the hotel fronting Cheapside, with plans of the basement, ground floor, first floor, second floor and attic. The plan for the ground floor shows, on the left, the *Entrance Hall, Bar, Bar-Parlour, Guild Room, Snug, Kitchen, Larder, Luggage Room, and Billiard Room*. Beyond that, were a *Groom's Pantry, Groom's Kitchen*, and a number of loose boxes or stalls. To the right of the front entrance was a passageway, partly covered, and a note on the plan which states '*First Floor of Hotel over here*'. Beyond this covered part the passage widened out to include a wealth of loose boxes, stables, and a harness room.

The first floor contained *the Rawstorne Room, Commercial Room, Albert Room, and Victoria Room,* which was separated from the large *Dining Room* by a *Movable Screen*; an arrangement which obviously held the possibility of making an extremely large dining room when required. There was a laundry, toilets, a bath room, three bedrooms, numbered 1, 2, 3, and what appears to be a large bedroom with accommodation for two grooms.

On the second floor were bedrooms numbered 5 – 22, and in the attic one more bedroom *'over Number 13'*, with a closet on the landing outside.

Seeing this plan I am conscious of a serious omission in my description of Castle Chambers, for here there was no ground floor accommodation; one had to ascend a staircase to reach the first floor offices of the Refuge Assurance Co., our flat, and the room once occupied by the Football League. A second flight of stairs led to other rooms leased to various tenants, and from there, another short staircase led to the room which was once, possibly, the attic. What had been the ground floor of the *'Castle Hotel'* was occupied for many years by the *Cash Clothing Co.,* a tailor's shop for men and boys.

There came a day, of course, when even Castle Chambers ceased to exist, and that was after the *Lancashire Evening Post* moved its operation from Fishergate in 1989. To the right of *Castle Chambers* had been a narrow thoroughfare leading from Cheapside to the premises of the *L.E.P.* down which their red vans had passed for years to collect newspapers from the presses for onward delivery. After a delay of three years when the Fishergate site was redeveloped, changes took place in Cheapside which saw *Castle Chambers* replaced by shops.

JOHN HOLKER

John Holker was elected M.P. for Preston in 1872, holding the seat in the elections of 1874 and 1880. He was born at Bury in 1828 and was a Norther Circuit barrister based in Manchester. Through his appearance – *"a tall, plain, lumbering Lancastrian"*, he was nicknamed *"Sleepy Jack"*. Holker wasn't "behind the door" though. He had moved to London, became a specialist in patent law and appeared in the famous *"Tichborne Claimant"* case in the year he became Preston's M.P. Subsequently, Disraeli appointed him Solicitor-General, then, following a knighthood, Attorney-General. Not so sleepy.

A PRESTON BUSINESS BUILT ON TICK

Bob Dobson

Victoria had been a Queen for six years when, in 1843, Thomas Yates established a watch-making business at 159 Friargate. He had been apprenticed to Mr Banks, a Fishergate watch-maker, and was twenty-nine years old when he started his enterprise. (Some sources suggest the business started in 1840).

Five years later, in 1848, he patented a watch mechanism which relied upon a minimum of movement, and therefore very little wear on the main spring and moving parts. He called it *"The Dead-Beat"* watch, and it soon brought him fame and custom from men throughout the world who wanted a reliable, durable watch.

At that time, Prince Albert was president of the Society for the Encouragement of Arts, Manufacturers and Commerce, and he received one of Thomas' watches. Thomas subsequently appeared before the Society's council and was commended for his contribution to the construction of lever watches. He received their certificate and silver medal.

Thomas employed skilled workmen in the various departments of his business, which soon developed into a leading jewellery business.

About 1919, when the firm was in the hands of Thomas' daughter, Emma, then in her sixties, it was sold to James Rhodes. He was a watchmaker and jeweller with a small business in Church Street and a reputation as an active temperance worker. The transaction was conditional upon Thomas Yates being kept as the firm's trading name.

In 1945, James' son Roger took over the business, which was then run from a leased property at 12 Friargate. It later passed to Roger's son, David, who bought the freehold of a small shop no. 33 Market Place in 1983. This is the family firm's shop today.

This property is perhaps the oldest shop property in Preston, having been in existence since at least 1580, and probably before that. It is no pun to describe this half- timbered jeweller's shop as a gem. It is thought that the pre-1600 roof beams have been covered in thatch, then corrugated iron, before today's slates were put on. It is a Grade II listed building, preserved and protected by today's members of the Rhodes family. David Rhode's son Charles, is the fourth generation watchmaker and jewellerworker in it.

Thomas Yates's silver medal and Royal Warrant are on display in the shop still bearing his name over the door, but the Rhodes family are still searching for the certificate which originally accompanied it.

THE LEA GATE

On Monday 28th July 1902, the private toll bar belonging to the De Hoghton Trustees at Lea Gate was abolished and the length of road in which it was situated declared free and open, part of the new main road from Blackpool to Preston. The ceremony should have taken place on the previous Monday but was delayed *"owing to some difficulty between the County Council and the tenant"*.

Read about the turnpikes, highways and byways in *"Leading the Way : a history of Lancashire's roads"* by Dr Alan Crosby (1998 Lancashire County Books).

Five examples of Preston firms displaying their specialities in pictorial form on their invoice. If you have summat to swank about ......

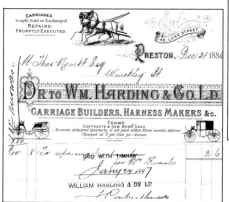

A 1903 view of Fishergate, one of the finest streets in the industrial north. The principal building is fishergate Baptist church, admired by Ruskin for the naturalistic detail on its facade. In the distance can be seen the wedge-shaped tower of Preston Gas Offices, and beyond it the old Town Hall of 1862-7. (Stephen Sartin)

This photo of Market Square about 1954 shows three of the principal buildings of nineteenth- century Preston. To the left is the Harris Free Library, Museum and Art Gallery, built in the classical style and completed in 1891. Centrally placed is the Miller Arcade, Preston's equivalent of *Harrod's,* built in late 1890's using the American steel frame system. On the right is the old Town Hall, built 1862-7 in the *"hotel de ville"* style. Sadly we see it without its great bell tower which fronted the Fishergate side and was demolished following a catastrophic fire on the Ides of March, 1947. (Stephen Sartin)

ALICE KIRBY – SHE SAW SIX GUILDS

Bob Dobson

The publication of this book in October 2003 marks the centenary of the death of a Preston centenarian – Such folk are quite remarkable today and certainly were so a hundred years ago.

Alice Saunderson was born at Elswick on 1st May 1799. Her father was a handloom weaver and worked on farms to feed his wife and children. Alice married at an early age young Christopher Kirby, who was also a handloom weaver and agricultural labourer. Their wedding was in Kirkham Parish Church. Their marriage was fruitful – they had ten children; five of each. Her husband died about 1858.

Due to her longevity and good health, Mrs Kirby became for several years one of the principal guests at the annual tea party held for Preston's old folk.

When interviewed on reaching her hundredth birthday (there was no mention of a telegram from the King), Alice was sprightly and in good fettle with some good teeth, good hearing and able to read without glasses. She had for some years been under the care of Dr King, though it would appear he had little to do. A journalist interviewing Alice at this time described her as being *"cant"* – a Lancashire dialect word meaning lively, active and cheerful.

To mark her centenary, the Mayor and Mayoress threw a party for Alice in the Public Hall. A great many of her descendants turned up and were photographed. There are fifty-odd relatives on the photo reproduced here, though a newspaper report of the time mentioned one with a hundred and twenty four descendants on. Alice is in the centre, wearing a shawl presented to her as a present by the Mayoress. Without doubt there are folk living in Preston today descended from this lady who lived through six Preston Guilds.

15, NORTH ROAD,
Preston, _July 27_ 190_3_

To FRED KIRBY, Jr.,
Practical Taxidermist and Naturalist.

Taxidermist to the Scottish Belle Vue, Glasgow, and to the Accrington Corporation Museums. Winner of Three Gold Medals (Highest Awards) for Taxidermy, 1893-4-5.
Heads of Prize Cattle, Horses, and Hoofs of favourite Horses mounted as Inkstands, Snuff-boxes, &c., in beautiful designs.—A Speciality.

'PRESTON LASSIES MUN HEV THE VOTE'

Patti Mayor, Artist and Suffragette

Greta Krypczyk-Oddy

On June 15th, 1908, Patti Mayor headed the large procession of women from Preston and other Lancashire towns in the *'Women's Sunday'* march in London; a demonstration which culminated in Hyde Park where platforms were set up and many speakers were listed to. This rally was organised by the *'Women's Social and Political Union (WSPU)'* and marked an important point in the Women's Suffrage movement. The Lancashire women walked behind Patti Mayor, who carried a portrait she had painted in 1906 entitled *The Half Timer,* which depicts a young girl wearing a shawl and carrying a tea can. Patti had painted this portrait in 1906 and her model was Annie Hill (later Annie Hunt) who at the time of sitting was a real *'half timer';* that is she worked for half a day at Horrockses Crewdons in Preston and for the other half of the day she went to school.

Patti indicated that her idea behind using this painting in the rally was to *'show London what was happening in Lancashire'* as well as depicting *'youth and beauty in a background of industry'.* This was a successful day for the WSPU, mainly because the decision to hold it on a Sunday meant that working women could attend as this was their day off. The special excursion trains which took women from Preston (and other parts of the country) were full.

Born in Preston in 1872 Patti Mayor trained in art at the Harris Institute in Preston and later in London. She also spent time in Paris, a city considered by some, (from the mid-nineteenth to the mid-twentieth century) to be the *'centre'* of the art world.

Fluent in French, she probably gained from this experience, as although her paintings are for the most part traditional in both style and composition, *'impressionistic'* brushstrokes are evident in some of her paintings. *"The Sewing Maid",* which is in the permanent collection of the Harris Art Galley in Preston is one which shows this influence.

Pattie and her sister Amy contributed to the Preston branch of the WSPU by organising and performing in several musical events over the period 1908 - 1914. Both sisters were trained in music and dance and Amy frequently gave piano recitals in Preston. One such recital was held in the Crush Room of the Public Hall in 1914 and included works by Beethoven, Grieg and Schumann. For a number of years Amy was music mistress at the Park School in Preston.

Patti's forte was painting and drawing. Throughout her long career as an artist she worked in a studio in Fishergate, Cheapside as well as at her home in Grosvenor Place, Ashton. In her sketch book dated 1958, she reflects on how much she enjoyed *'drawing human faces'* and how the *'most prolific'* part of her life was *'up to the war of 1914.'* This covers the period when the suffrage movement was at its height.

In the early 20th century she shared the Fishergate studio with Swiss born Frances Bentham, who taught at the Harris School. They held exhibitions in the studio and also purchased a *'ready-made'* art class (in Lytham), which consisted of 10-20 young ladies. Latterly, Patti continued this class alone in order to fund one or more of her trips to Paris. She apparently enjoyed this experience and took some of her pupils on *'sketching holidays'* and days out. Her sketch book reports of one day spent in Liverpool when she and her pupils visited the *'landing stage,'* viewing the *'big ships.'* Some sketches show her fascination for ships and their passengers and because Liverpool was easily reached by rail, the Transatlantic liners which docked there provided a wealth of material for her art and interest. Early sketches show this interest; as in 1894-5 when she drew some of fellow passengers on the deck of *SS Powerful,* which according to Lloyds Register was a *'wooden paddle steamer of 338 gross tons'* registered in Montreal in 1894.

Liverpool featured again in her career when she exhibited at the city's Walker Art Gallery, whose records list titles and some sale prices of works in this exhibition. These indicate variety in her work. The paintings exhibited include:
The Fan (1898) painted in oil offered for £3.3s. (£3.15p)
A Bit of Old Preston (1910) in pastel and water colour £3.10s (£3.50p)
and *A Child Study* (1904) £10.10s (10 guineas or £10.50p)

By selling her work through gallery exhibitions, studio exhibitions, teaching and taking on commissions demonstrates how she was able to earn her living as an artist at a time when few women did so. As with most other professions, art was predominantly a male domain but her dedication and talent secured her success.

The first militant act by the WSPU came in October, 1905 when Christabel Pankhurst and Annie Kenny disrupted a meeting of Liberal speakers in the Free Trade Hall in Manchester. Their refusal to pay fines led to imprisonment. Edith Rigby of Winckley Square, Preston, joined WSPU soon afterwards and on February 28th, 1907 she placed a letter in the *Lancashire Daily Post* headed *'Votes for Women'*. This letter declared the *'Annie Kenny is to visit Preston next week'* and along with Edith Rigby, wife of Dr. Charles Rigby, would address a meeting held on Preston's Market Square. This combination was successful in attracting women from all social backgrounds to join the movement and soon after this meeting the Preston branch of the WSPU was set up.

'Votes for Women' was not the only issue on the agenda and other topics included higher education, access to the professions, as well as married women's rights over property and childcare. These were some of the issues which affected women of all classes. By 1908 the Preston WSPU had offices and held meetings in a room above a tea merchant's premises at 41, Glovers Court, Preston; Edith Rigby was Secretary and a Miss Ainsworth of Ribbleton was Treasurer. Other members included Patti and Amy Mayor, Grace Alderman of Broadgate, Mrs R. Towler of Manchester Road, Mrs Hesmondhalgh of Dove Street and Mrs and Miss Pass of Broughton Post Office. Patti Mayor died in 1962 and commemorative exhibitions of her work have been held since: one was at the end of 1963 at the Harris in Preston and another was at the Grundy Art Galley in Blackpool in 1988. An article in the *Lancashire Evening Post* of June 22nd, 1988 states the ' *The Artist (Patti Mayor) took the identity of her models to the grave'* and curators of the Grundy exhibition were hoping that relatives of the models may come forward and identify some of the *'mysterious faces'*. It is not clear if any were identified but what is certain is that Patti Mayor painted and drew for about 80 of her 91 years. A Christian Scientist, a vegetarian and earning her living as an artist all suggest non-conformist and her work and comments on her pupils 'work reflects this. Paintings which are technically fine and detailed, portraits

enigmatic and sensitive suggest that, alongside some work by other female artists of the period, Patti Mayor has not yet received the acclaim she deserves.

As well as depicting how child labour was still considered appropriate in the cotton mills of Preston less than a century ago Patti Mayor's portrait of *The Half Timer* played a major part in the history of Preston's pioneer women and could possibly be viewed as her most important work.

Paintings, drawings and sketches by Patti Mayor can be seen in the Harris in Preston and the Grundy in Blackpool. Other works are held in private collections.

* * * * *

Wanted.

PRESTON UNION.

MALE IMBECILE ATTENDANT.

The Guardians of the above Union Require the Services of a Male Imbecile Attendant for the Ribchester Workhouse. The person appointed will be required to perform such other reasonable duties as the Master of the Workhouse may appoint. Candidates, who must be between 35 and 45 years of age, are requested to see the Master of the Ribchester Workhouse and ascertain the nature of the duties required from them. Salary, £20 per annum, with board, lodging, and washing.

Applications, in the handwriting of the applicant, together with copies only of testimonials, must be made on forms to be obtained from the undersigned, and must reach me not later than Wednesday, the 3rd January next.

JAMES CLARKE,
Clerk to the Guardians.

Union Offices, Preston,
20th December, 1905.

STOP THAT OPERATION.

CONSULT NURSE SLATER

(Of North-road, Lancaster), HERNIA SPECIALIST.
TO-MORROW (WEDNESDAY), February 12th,
At 15, CANNON-STREET, PRESTON.
Hours of Attendance, 11 15 a.m. until 5 p.m.

NURSE SLATER will be in attendance To-morrow (Wednesday), at 15, Cannon-street, Preston. Nurse Slater's skill in all Internal Diseases of Women has been proved by thousands. She is still pursuing her mission against the use of inward instruments. Ruptures and Women's Inward Weaknesses Cured without operation or inward instruments. Advice Free.

EDMUND ROBERT HARRIS, PRESTON'S GREATEST PUBLIC BENEFACTOR

Tom Smith

Undoubtedly the finest building in the centre of Preston is the Harris Library and Museum designed by James Hibbert. Overlooking the Market Square it has become the centre of many civic and festive occasions since its official opening in 1893. Like several other institutions across the city, its existence is the result of a large amount of money bequeathed by Edmund Robert Harris on his death in May 1877. At the time it amounted to £300,768, an enormous sum, and approximately £14 millions in today's figures. Despite his generosity, he was neither a public figure during his lifetime nor has he become famous since his death. The reason may be because only one small portrait painted in 1830 and no photographs of him are known to exist. During his lifetime he took no part in the social life of the area and when he retired he became a semi-recluse.

Edmund Robert Harris was born in 1803 the second son of Robert Harris of Clitheroe who had married a Preston woman, Nancy Lodge. Robert had been educated at Clitheroe Grammar School and Cambridge University and became the curate of St. George's Chapel, Preston, in 1797 as well as the headmaster of the Free Grammar School. Robert and Nancy had four children: Robert who died in infancy, Edmund Robert, Thomas and Ellen Elizabeth. He was a well liked, quiet and unpretentious clergyman who eventually died at the age of 97 in January 1862 having preached his last sermon in St. George's Chapel as recently as the preceding Christmas Day.

The family spent their early years in the house of the Free Grammar School in Stoneygate which had been built in 1728. This later became famous because Richard Arkwright, in one of its back rooms, developed his spinning machine in 1768. Apart from being the residence of headmasters and their families it has since had a variety of uses, including being a public house known as the Arkwright Arms, an education centre in the 1980s and, at present, the office of Age Concern. It is likely that Edmund Robert was educated at the Grammar School and its connection with the Harris name was ensured when in 1877 he left an endowment of £3000 to provide scholarships for the benefit of its pupils. The old school buildings were eventually closed in 1841 because the Stoneygate locality had become one of the poorer parts of the town and a move took place to new buildings in Cross Street.

On leaving school, the Harris brothers went into the legal profession and were articled to their uncles, Edmund and Jonathan Lodge in Chapel Street. Both uncles were bachelors and when they retired Edmund Robert and Thomas took over the firm as partners. Meanwhile their father retired from the headship of the Grammar School in 1835 and eventually as vicar of St. George's in 1862. The family by then had moved to No.13 Ribblesdale Place which is occupied by the present Vicar of Preston.

None of the Harris children married. Ellen Elizabeth apparently discouraged the advances of one suitor because he could not ride on horseback. Little is known about the family save a few reminiscences written by Sir Charles Brown, a consultant surgeon at Preston Royal Infirmary and who died in 1925 aged 89 years. His notes were only discovered in the 1970s attached to the house deeds of No.13 and in them he described how he remembered the two brothers and their sister riding on horseback to their stables in Garden Street, off Chapel Street. Of Thomas he wrote that *"He was reported at the Winckley Club to exercise great economy in the purchase of his cigars; they were said to be of a very inferior quality and he puffed into the billiard room rather an unpleasant aroma."* He described Edmund as *"very nervous and when excited the angle of his mouth spasmodically nearly touched his ear"*. This affliction might well have accounted for his shy and retiring personality, lack of social involvement and why he generally avoided portraiture. There is, however, a bust of Ellen Elizabeth in the Harris Art Gallery and an engraving of their father, Rev. Robert Harris.

In business Edmund was careful and conscientious to an extreme and reputed to be more than necessarily cautious. Everything had to be done with the strictest form and propriety and in complete accordance with the letter of the law. It was this attention to detail, thorough application and exactness, together with his integrity and reliability, which earned him a highly respected reputation. In 1848 he was appointed *'Deputy Prothonotary'* for Lancashire which meant that he was an assistant to the chief clerk or registrar in the Court of Common Pleas at Lancaster. By 1869 he had become the prothonotary for the county, an office which he held until retirement five years later.

Shortly after the death of their father in 1862 Edmund and Thomas moved to *"Whinfield"* in Whinfield Lane, Ashton, pleasantly situated overlooking the Ribble. It was a large residence where they lived in some style for it included a dining room, drawing room, library, smoke room, several bedrooms and dressing rooms together with their servants' quarters. There was also a cellar said to have contained over five hundred dozen bottles of the choicest wines. Despite this luxury Edmund nevertheless remained a man of simple tastes and was always regarded by his servants as a kind and considerate master. During his later years he became afflicted by bronchitis and other problems of old age though he remained a regular attender at St. Andrew's Church in Ashton. In 1875 his brother Thomas died. Edmund Robert also passed away on 27th May 1877.

When he died he was a very wealthy man. He was the last survivor of the Harris and Lodge families and the sole inheritor from his parents, his uncles, his brother and his sister. In addition to a good income from his work in the legal profession he had invested shrewdly, both in real estate and in railway stocks which were booming in the middle of the 19th century. He owned land in several areas including Liverpool, Kendal, Ribchester and Preston, together with properties in different parts of the county. These included the *'Rose and Crown'* at Much Hoole which he bequeathed to Edward Bradley, who was formerly his clerk.

During his lifetime it was known by friends that Edmund rarely turned down a request for assistance and when a ward for infectious diseases was needed at the local infirmary he immediately donated £7000. Shortly before he died Edmund had told Thomas Edelston, later Mayor of Preston , and for twenty-two years a solicitor with the Harris firm, that the bulk of his fortune would be left to charity. His will stated that the money should be used *"to establish or build and endow a convalescent hospital, or orphanage, or almshouses, or literary or scientific institutions, or free library, or all of them, or any other charitable institution or institution of public utility which the trustees may think fit and proper and which may contribute to perpetuate the remembrance of my father and his family in the town."*

Within fifteen years of his death the trustees of the Harris bequest had spent over £300,000. The Harris Free Public Library and Art Museum was opened in 1893, when Thomas Edelston was Mayor, at a cost of £76,609. A further £22,947 was spent on objects of art and the contents of the reference library and £18,877 given as an endowment. £100,000 went on the Harris Orphanage, £70,000 for the Harris Institute and the provision of technical education, £6,335 for various churches and schools, and £3,000 was used for scholarships at Preston Grammar School.

Edmund Robert Harris died as he had always lived, a Christian gentleman. His money was left not to perpetuate his own memory nor his benevolence but in the hope that his father and the family would be remembered by future Prestonians. How successful this has been is hard to assess. Certainly no other person in the long history of the borough has shown anything like the same generosity to their fellow citizens as he did.

Edmund Robert Harris.
Reproduced by permission of the Keeper of Fine Arts,
The Harris Museum and Art Gallery.

Map showing proposed site of Library & Museum

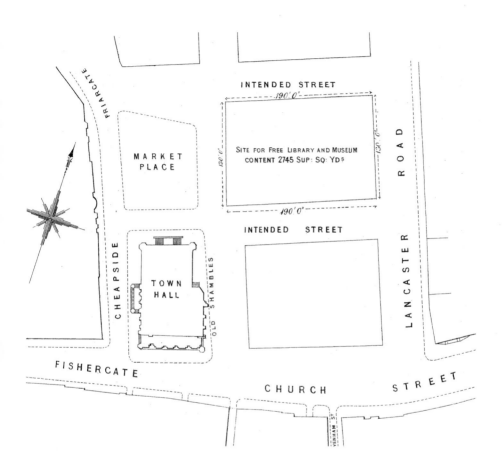

The *Illustrated London News* artist drew this for his paper at the time of the 1882 Guild. The caption referred to it being a **Free** Library and Museum-a relatively new concept in those times. It was designed, built and paid for by Preston men. The artist was portraying it from the architect's (Councillor James Hibbert) design. The ceremony of laying the foundation stone was performed on the Tuesday of Guild week. The building would be officially opened five years later.

This man had a stake in Preston - no bones about it. The 1908 photo shows Thomas Rainford, who came from a family of butchers, outside his shop at 30 Fishergate. He advertised that he had corned beef, pickled tongues, beef and pork sausages *"always on hand"*. He delivered orders *"to all parts of Preston and surrounding district"*. Equally impressive as his stock was his early use of the telephone. How did he get that *"cherished number"?* Research reveals that Thomas, just a few years earlier, had the number 0599 and it wasn't until 1938 that it was changed to 2831. By that time, Thomas had opened more butcher's chops, grocery shops and a restaurant in the town. He owned farms at Myerscough, Lea and Blackpool and was president of the Preston Master Butchers Association. In 1923 he became Conservative Councillor and in 1932/2 Mayor - not bad for a lad educated at St Thomas'. He took pride on the scale of his farming, his buying of only locally reared stock and the thousands he spent with local farmers.

THE TULLIS BROTHERS

Derek Wrathall

Whilst the architects of many of Preston's historic buildings are well known, the men who brought the architect's plans into reality are unsung, yet without their skills those plans could not have been translated into the fine buildings which are still with us.

Three Tullis brothers, Alexander (1819-91), David (1822-1902) and James (1824-1901) played a significant part in the creation of the Preston townscape.

They were all born at Cupar, Fife, but, following the death of their father, their mother moved to Preston in 1834, probably to be near her brother, David Fitchie, a master mason living and working here.

Clearly guided by his uncle, Alexander was apprenticed to a Preston stonemason. This would last seven years and he would then become a journeyman mason on becoming twenty one. Six years later (1845), he joined his younger brother, James, then not quite out of a similar apprenticeship, and a friend, William Cooper, to start the firm of **Cooper & Tullis.** The three young men took over the business of Mr. Bond, who had been their employer.

David was working on a farm before deciding to join his mother in Preston. He travelled by canal from Edinburgh to Glasgow, then by steamer to Liverpool before taking a coach to Preston. He worked for a couple of years with his uncle, David, presumably as a labourer, before becoming apprenticed to another Preston mason,

James Huddleston. When trade was slack, Huddleston laid off his journeymen but kept young David on. When his two brothers were setting up their partnership with William Cooper, David was travelling the country looking for work. He estimated that he had walked almost 1600 miles before returning to Preston.

Cooper & Tullis prospered. They moved premises within the town, employed men and became slate merchants. They were able, through keeping a good stock of stone and employing good craftsmen, to take on big contracts which included the building of St. Walburge's Church, the Town Hall, the Railway Station, the Harris Museum and Library, Whittingham Asylum, Churnclough Reservoir and Bolton Parish Church.

William Cooper died in 1859, but the brothers kept on their established name. They employed David for some years as yard manager and his son, Alexander, also worked for the firm, as did the son of Alexander senior, Ashton Alexander.

In 1872, David left his brothers to found his own firm, **David Tullis & Son**, along with his eldest lad, William. Alexander, a younger son, later joined them and the firm became **David Tullis & Sons**. They too prospered, being able to take on work such as the building of the County Quarter Sessions House. This family firm was to last until 1905.

Alexander Tullis   David Tullis   James Tullis

Reputation; A Firm Foundation

In 1890, the eldest brother, Alexander, became president of the *"Preston Master Builders Association"*. David's eldest lad, William, was also on the committee of this body, as was, at a later time, young Alexander who also became president in 1904. The Association was to become the *"Preston & District Building Trade Employers Association"*. The Tullis family were held in high regard by their peers in the trade and by the townspeople. The brothers went to different churches and chapels, and held differing political views, but were as one in their values of industry, integrity and quality workmanship.

The Tullis name lives on. The University of Central Lancashire acknowledges the contribution of the brothers in the presentation of *"The Tullis Award"* to a successful student in a degree course in the Department of Built Environment.

* * * * * *

Was *"Life"* his real name? One doesn't see much life in a cemetery. This advert appeared in a preston booklet in 1895. There are no subscribers listed under *"Life"* in the present-day telephone directory. Perhaps they are all dead - lifeless!

William Harrison Ashworth, "The Lancashire Novelist"

Preston 1715: A Victorian Novelist's View

His name is not familiar to the majority of readers today, but one of the most successful novelists of the early Victorian age was William Harrison Ainsworth. Born and educated in Manchester, Ainsworth found fame and, for a time, fortune in the London literary world of the 1830s and 40s. Of his forty novels, seven were based on Lancashire stories, the best known of these being *The Lancashire Witches* (1849), a tale built upon Thomas Potts's account of the Lancaster witch trials of 1612. This was published at the height of the author's fame, when his popular acclaim rivalled even that of Dickens, and it remains the only title to have been constantly in print up to the present day.

The latter part of Ainsworth's career saw a fall from grace as public tastes moved away from the historical romance, to favour the kind of domestic realism typified by Trollope and Thackeray. Unable or unwilling to adapt to these changes in reading fashion, Ainsworth continued to write novels based on historical themes, for ever-lower remuneration. In 1875, *Preston Fight* was published for a fraction of the fees commanded by his earlier works, but the novel shows no sign of the author's economic straits, being written with all the style and energy which characterises

Ainsworth's best work. The main story follows the course of the Jacobite Rebellion of 1715 from Scotland through Northumberland, Cumberland and Lancaster, culminating in the engagement at Preston and the subsequent fate of the insurgents. For the factual basis of this part of the story, Ainsworth consulted a volume published by the Chetham Society in 1845, entitled *The state of the parties in Lancashire before the rebellion of 1715,* by Dr Samuel Hibbert Ware. This includes an eye-witness description of the conflict, and the events surrounding it, written by Peter Clarke, an attorney's clerk from Kendal, under the heading: *'Preston Fight'.*

In several of his novels, Ainsworth's technique was to take such a factual account, and weave around it a series of stories, intrigues and sub-plots, adding fictional characters and imaginary scenarios to the historical facts. These are supported and interspersed with convincingly detailed descriptive passages, resulting in a spicy mixture of fact and fiction, driven along by the author's relentless narrative pace. *Preston Fight* is an excellent example of this technique. Divided into eleven sections or *'Books',* the progress of the insurgents is traced from place to place until, in Book VII, Chapter 1, the rebel army at last reaches Preston. Entitled 'Proud Preston'. This chapter opens with an introduction to the town and its people:

> *Proud Preston – or Priest's Town as it was originally called from the number of its religious houses – merited the epithet applied to it, albeit somewhat derisively.*
>
> *Proud were its inhabitants – proud of their town – of its fine situation, its beauty, its salubrity – proud of their wives and daughters, whom they deemed, and not erroneously, the handsomest women in the Kingdom. As a place of fashionable resort, where the best society could be found, Preston, at the period of our story, ranked higher than any other town in the North of England. A great number of gentry resided there – many of them belonging to the oldest Catholic families in the country, and these persons gave an aristocratic character to the place.*
>
> *But the Preston gentry were not as wealthy as they were proud. High churchmen as well as Roman Catholics abounded in then town, and the only thing low about the parish church was the steeple.*

Hence the old rhyme:
Proud Preston, poor people,
High church and low steeple!

Thus the scene is set for the hostilities which were to follow. We have a town divided along sectarian lines, shortly to be occupied by rebel forces. While the aristocratic catholic families might be expected to support the Jacobite insurgents, Ainsworth is careful to point out that opposition could be expected from the Anglicans. Chief among these is the Reverend Samuel Peploe, vicar of Preston, who is described as *'a staunch supporter of the reigning family and greatly opposed to the Jacobites.'* The reference to the 'wives and daughters' of the town is justified by a line in Peter Clarke's original report of the situation. One of the mysteries of the 1715 rebellion is that, having reached Preston, the insurgents were aware of the loyal forces massing at Wigan, under the command of General Wills. Instead of pressing on to a more advantageous tactical position at Manchester or Chester, the Jacobites chose to linger in Preston, where they were vulnerable to attack, and were ultimately defeated.

Peter Clarke's explanation of the conduct was all too human:
> *The Ladys in this toune, Preston, are so very beautifully & so richly atired, that the Gentlemen soldiers from Wednesday to Saturday minded nothing but courting and ffeasting.*

Hibbert Ware fleshes out this statement, picturing the condition of the men on reaching Preston:
> *To take a generous view of the affair, - "The Gentlemen Soldiers", fatigued with the hunger, the thirst, the long marches, the watchings, the painful anxieties, and the other toils of a perilous expedition, seemed to have enjoyed, with so much greater zest, the hospitality of Preston, and the entertainments prepared for them by the assiduity of the fair Lancashire witches.*

Much is made of this idea in Ainsworth's novel. He introduces a beautiful spy, Mrs Scarisbrick, who beguiles General Forster, the commander of the rebel forces, and helps to bring about his defeat.

Ainsworth has been described as *'a prime exponent of the potent concept of Merry*

England.' To the Victorians, this represented a notion of an idyllic, pre-industrial time, based on traditional pursuits and centred upon rural rather than urban life. The description of the town of Preston in Ainsworth's novel is unashamedly nostalgic, looking back to a romantic vision of an earlier age with a relish that is the privilege of the historical novelist:

> *Delightfully situated on the summit of a ridge, rising gradually from the Ribble, which sweeps round it on the south, and commanding extensive and beautiful views in every direction, Preston, from its salubrious climate, and contiguity to the sea, enjoyed the reputation of being one of the most agreeable and healthy towns in England.*
>
> *In the early part of the eighteenth century Preston was but a small place, and could boast little regularity of construction, but it had a remarkably clean and cheerful aspect.*
>
> *Attached to many of the houses were good gardens, and these being laid out on the slopes of the eminence on which the town was reared, contributed materially to its beauty.*
>
> *In the market place, which formed a large square, with an obelisk in the midst instead of a cross, there were several good old houses, and here, also was the town hall, an extremely picturesque old edifice, four stories high, and each story projecting above the other, painted black and white, and having great gables and large windows.*
>
> At the corner of one of the streets communicating with the market-place stood the Mitre, the principal hostel of the town, and *noted for its good cheer and good wines. Not far off was the White Bull, another good inn, much frequented by the townsfolk...Such was the Preston when garrisoned by the insurgent forces.*

This is a picture of a clean, airy town whose centre is dominated by an ancient market square, which would also have been its commercial heart, where farmers would come to sell their produce. In returning to the eighteenth century, Ainsworth evokes a vision untainted by the industrialisation that characterised the age in which he lived. A very different portrait of Preston had been produced more than twenty years earlier by Charles Dickens, Ainsworth's friend and near contemporary, in *Hard Times* (1854), when *'Coketown'* (Dickens's pseudonym for Preston) was depicted as follows:

It was a town of machinery and tall chimneys, out of which interminable serpents of smoke trailed themselves for ever and ever, and never got uncoiled. It had a black canal in it, and a river that ran purple with ill-smelling dye, and vast piles of building full of windows where there was a rattling and a trembling all day long, and where the piston of the steam-engine worked monotonously up and down, like the head of an elephant in a state of melancholy madness.

The contrast between Dickens's bleak portrait of ninteenth-century Preston and Ainsworth's idyllic vision of the town in 1715 could not have been starker. The river has become polluted, the climate is no longer *'salubrious',* and the *'clean and cheerful aspect'* has given way to smoke, grime, noise and misery. One similarity between these two views of the town is that Dickens's Preston, like Ainsworth's was a town in the throes of conflict, but this time it was the inequities between employers and workers that exercised the novelist's mind.

Unfortunately, *Preston Fight* failed to revive Ainsworth's flagging career. The reading public was not about to regain its appetite for the romantic nostalgia and swashbuckling action of this type of historical novel. William Harrison Ainsworth died in January 1882, almost seven years (and six novels) later. He had retired to relative, but not uncomfortable ,obscurity, emerging briefly to receive a late accolade from his native city, in the form of a civic banquet in the new Manchester Town Hall, when he declared himself proud to be known as 'The Lancashire Novelist'. Despite its lack of success and renown, *Preston Fight* remains a fine example of its genre and an exciting evocation of the events centred on Preston in 1715. It is well worth searching the second-hand bookshops for a copy of this supremely entertaining book.

NO CONTEST

Robert Ingham

When I were a lad and watched footba'
Why, we went off to t'match and had fun –
Exceptin' for a' them occasions
On which t'other buggers had won.

Now, t'team I supported were Preston,
Aye, we shouted for t'famous North End
And in that there team were a player
On who tha could allus depend.

His name – say it soft – were Tom Finney,
And give it aw t'reverence that's due
To a chap as could turn on a tanner
And beat anyone – any two.

He could dribble his way down yon right wing
And centre from t'bye-line, tha knows,
Then he'd do it again o'er on t'left side
And stick ba' in t'net to applause.

Nay, they had a good team in them days, lad,
They were Langton and Wayman an' aw
And Docherty playin' at half-back;
By the heck, they were wick, they could go!

Now, sometimes we went to watch Blackpoo',
They were just t'other way along t'road,
And they had a fella ca'd Matthews
As some reckoned were good – What a fraud!

His left leg were nobbut to stan' on,
He weren't able to head ba' nor score,
When he felt cowd he'd dribble down t'touchline
And bang o'er a few centres, nowt more.

Anyway, he kept playin' for England
(They were reet silly buggers at t'top)
So they had to put Finney on t'left wing
Because Stanley weren't able to swap.

So, tha sees, it were really no contest,
Tha cannot compare ale and watter,
Ee, them experts they make me feel badly
Wi' a' their continual natter.

When they're chunnerin' on about craftsmen
And they tell thee that Matthews were great.
Tha mun answer that next to Tom Finney
He could on'y be ca'd t'plumber's mate.

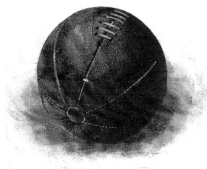

The " Embee " Button End or Capless Ball.
9/6 EACH. THREE FOR 27/-, POST FREE.

EMBEE *STANDS FOR*

Merigold Bros.,

SPORTS' OUTFITTERS,

147, CHURCH-ST.,

PRESTON.

CYCLE REPAIRERS, ENAMELLERS, AND PLATERS.

Large Stock of Playing Cards.

THE HARRIS - A BOWLER HAT ON A PEDESTAL

Bob Dobson

In October 1940, something occurred in the Harris Museum and Art Gallery, which had not occurred previously, and I doubt has occurred since:- a man fell to his death 45 feet from the second floor to the ground.

William Phillips, a 77 year old retired stage manager fell – or did he jump? – over the three-feet high balustrade. Evidence was given that 5ft 4ins tall Mr Phillips suffered from rheumatism and had attacks of dizziness.

The Inquest, reported in the Lancashire Evening Post, was told by Det. Sgt. Wilson that Mr Phillips' bowler hat was found on a pedestal on the second floor. Had he taken it off and put it there? There appears to have been no evidence from a pathologist as to cause of death, such as might be deduced from the condition of his heart.

No noise had been heard, such as a protest from Mr Phillips, nor was any mention made of anyone else being on the second floor at that time. His son believed that, as his father had plenty of time on his hands, he was probably looking around the museum, even though climbing the seventy five steps would have been difficult or arduous for him.

An "Open" verdict was recalled. Agatha Christie could have written a whole book around the tale of this death where there is usually a deathly silence.

THOMAS DUCKETT & THOMAS DUCKETT
PRESTON SCULPTORS

Thomas Duckett is a name to be revered in Preston – doubly so, for this father and son brought notice and honour to the town. There's no street named after them, nor do their statues grace the town – well, that's not strictly true. Read on.

Thomas Duckett (Senior) was born locally in 1803 and came from farming stock. He was bound apprentice to a plasterer making the models for the fancy plasterwork fashionable in Georgian and Victorian houses. However, he sought work of a more artistic nature and arranged to be freed from his indenture to take up work as a wood carver in the world-famous Gillow company in Lancaster. From there he moved to Liverpool to work in a marble sculptor's workshop. Though new to this field, he showed great promise and in no time at all was *"head-hunted"* by Messrs. Webster of Kendal, perhaps the most reputable firm of sculptors in the land. He became a departmental manager.

In this capacity he carved a group *"of heroic size and full relief"* of St George and the Dragon for a Kendal Catholic Church. The local limestone was notoriously brittle and the finished product of his self-imposed task from his own design was described as *"Herculean"*, all done with mallet and chisel.

Soon afterwards he returned to Preston, living in Cannon Street and working from a studio in Avenham Road.

Thomas executed work for customers throughout he land – group sculptures and busts, but his masterpiece was erected just around the corner in Winckley Square – Sir Robert Peel. When seen by that great man's son, he remarked how well the sculptor had *"caught"* his father's facial expression and stance. Thomas also designed and executed a colossal statue of Sir Richard Arkwright seated, but failed to find a customer to pay for its construction in stone or bronze and had to demolish it. About 1870, Thomas designed and sculpted the trulymagnificent, forty-feet high marble altar in St Augustine's Church, Frenchwood, which over a century later, with the church closed since 1984, is in danger of being lost to the town through the economics of available space and dwindling number of suitable repositories.

Thomas was a gifted painter too, though he admitted to having shortcomings as a draughtsman. Shortcomings or not, he taught art at the Preston School of Art and laboured to introduce art in its widest context into the lives of Prestonians, being a member of the council of the Institute for the Diffusion of Knowledge. He died in 1878.

Twice married, his eldest son became a vicar, another son and one of his daughters became art teachers, but young Thomas (born 1839 in Kendall) went on to emulate his esteemed father, though to a lesser degree. He studied art at the Royal Academy in London. To further his knowledge and skills, he took his new wife to Rome, but found it difficult to earn a living and returned to London.

Throughout his married life, and perhaps before it, young Thomas had poor health – a constant cough and chest pains. His doctors diagnosed *"consumption"* – we would call it *"tuberculosis"*. There were no drugs to cure it, and Thomas was advised to take a long sea voyage. They don't come any longer than to Australia, so he set off for that place in the hope of finding sunshine to ease his lungs and work to feed the pregnant wife and child he had to leave behind. A family friend, sculptress Mrs Pearson of Newton in Cartmel gave him financial assistance.

The doctors in Melborne could not help pale-faced Thomas. There was little work for an artist or a sculptor, even though he had moved to live in Tasmania before returning to Sydney in 1867. There his luck turned, though his health didn't. This forced him to live *"in the bush"* in a tent. He had no liking for the Aussies.

Even though, with the patronage of the Governor's wife, Thomas got more work, he was often too weak to attend to it through the constant coughing-up of blood. Depression hit him, especially when he received a letter to say that his wife had died. He too died, aged just twenty nine years, in April 1868. Four life-sized angels, modelled by Thomas, guard the entrance of the Sydney cemetery where he was buried.

THE TOTAL ABSTINENCE SOCIETY: NO HALF MEASURES

Bob Dobson

There had been great feeling expressed throughout the country for some time about the evils of alcoholic drinks when, in August 1832, John King and Joseph Livesey met in Livesey's Preston cheese shop. They discussed the movement towards getting people to denounce *"drink"* for good, not for a limited period.

Livesey wrote down a promise, or pledge which read *"We agree to abstain from all liquors of an intoxicating quality, whether ale, porter, wine or ardent spirits – except as medicine".*

King signed it first, then Livesey, before deciding to call a special meeting of members of the *Total Abstinence Society* in The Cockpit, Stonygate, on Saturday 1st September. This was to become the *Preston Temperance Society's* home for the next twenty years and known as *"The Temperance Hall".*

At this meeting, the *"pledge"* prepared by King and Livesey was discussed and signed by five others – John Gratrix, Edward Dickinson, John Broadbent, John Smith and David Anderton. This group of advocates became known as *"the Seven Men of Preston"* and their action on that day came to be seen as a momentuous moment within the history of the Temperance Movement which has such strong links with Preston.

A Pledge Certificate issued by a St Helens "Band of Hope" (Temperance) Society.

It has to be said that not all of the magnificent seven kept to their word, and that others contributed more to the battle against boozc. Amongst this larger group, many were "*reformed drunkards*".

To study the Temperance Movement in Preston is to learn much about social ills in the country and of political manoeuvrings and chisms within a large organisation.

Many fine Prestonians feature on the big canvas, not least amongst them Richard

"*Dickie*" Turner, born at Bilsborrow in 1790. He was a reformed drunkard with little education. It is said that Dickie stammered hesitancy over the word "*total*", giving repeated emphasis on the initial "*t*", created the word "*teetotal*". That may have been a cruel jibe at his affliction, but it is a good story which today's publicists would give an arm and a leg for.

In 1846, soon before he died, Dickie walked to London and back to attend the World Temperance Convention, recommending the cause to all who were attracted to the sound of his rattle.

ANTHONY HEWITSON :
JOURNALIST AND HISTORIAN

Bob Dobson

Although born in Blackburn in 1836, Anthony Hewitson always considered the Yorkshire Dales village of Ingleton as his native place. He was the son of another Anthony Hewitson, a stonemason, and his wife Alice, and when young Anthony was ready for school he was sent to live in Ingleton with his maternal (Moor) grandparents.

He attended the village school and lived the life of a typical village lad for the next ten years, leaving in 1850, now 14 years old, to take up an apprenticeship as a journalist/reporter with the *"Lancaster Gazette"*. This decade of his life was important to him, and he was to make notes about it and contribute a series of articles about it in the *"Lancaster Standard"* in 1893 under the pen-name of *"Ingle"*.

These articles and the notebook were to be converted into book form in 1982 – *"The Story of My Village – Ingleton 1840-50"* and were published by John Bentley, a Burnley man with a love of Ingleton. It is a wonderful record of life in a Pennine village at that time. Later Hewitson would be praised by historian Joseph Carr for *"putting Ingleton on the map"*.

On becoming a journeyman at the end of his apprenticeship, Anthony left Lancaster to work on the *"Kendal Mercury"*, and later on a paper in Staffordshire.

1858 saw Hewitson, now a capable, time-served and much travelled newspaper man, return North to join the *"Preston Guardian"*, but a few months later he moved over to the *"Preston Chronicle"*, five years later he became manager of the *"Preston Herald"*, and later moved back to the *"Preston Guardian"* as chief reporter.

In March 1868, now steeped in knowledge of Preston, its movers and shakers and in the newspaper world, he bought the *"Preston Chronicle"*, becoming its editor and publisher.

Even though he travelled extensively in Europe and the United States, meeting several literary greats, Hewitson found the time to research and write books about his adopted home town and the area to its North. He edited and wrote several books which have become respected and sought after:- "*The Preston Court Leet Records*"; "*Preston, its Churches and Chapels*"; "*Our Country Churches*"; "*Preston Town Council – Portraits of Local Legislators*"; "*Stonyhurst College, its past and present*"; "*The Diary of Thomas Tyldesley*", "*A History of Preston*" and "*Northward*". This last one, and some others, he wrote under his pen-name of "*Atticus*". It is a masterpiece of writing about the area between Preston and Lancaster in the days before the motor car. Originally published in 1900, it has been recently been republished by *Landy Publishing*.

In 1890, the "*Preston Chronicle*" was purchased by the town's major newspaper force, the "*Preston Guardian*". It appears to mark the point at which Hewitson took a back seat so far as Preston journalism was concerned. He clearly continued to write and research and took an interest in the "*Dewsbury Chronicle*" which was (perhaps) owned by one of his two sons. He also had two daughters. For six years in the late 1880's he lived at a house called "*Brookhouse*", just south of the "*Green Man*" pub at Bilsborrow. He was to sell this to Isaac Simpson, a Preston manufacturer of gold thread.

He probably left Bilsborrow for Queens Road, Fulwood, and later, when wishing to live in a better climate, he moved to Prince's Crescent, Bare, Morecambe. He was said to be "*in very robust health*" until just before he died on 26th October, 1912. His coffin was carried on the train from Morecambe to Preston and he was buried in the Non-Conformist section of Preston cemetery. His funeral was conducted by Reverend Benjamin Nightingale, a major historian of the Non-Conformity in Lancashire. The two men would have known each other.

A bill sent by Hewitson, trading under his own name rather than that of the *"Preston Chronicle"* to Mr Nevett for an advert inserted in two issues of the paper. It took Nevett six months to pay the half a guinea charge.

* * * * * *

A PRESTON "FIRST"

On Christmas Eve 1832, the first Temperance Hotel in England – on total abstinence principles – was opened at the corner of Church Street and North Road.

ANOTHER

On 1st January 1834, Joseph Livesey published *"The Preston Temperance Advocate"* newspaper / magazine to spread the principle of Total Abstinence. Preston had become *"Britain's first source of the teetotal stream"*.

WHAT PRESTON DOES TODAY....

The French claim the invention, about 1630, of the paper making technique known as "marbling", which results in paper being given what might be called a pattern effect not unlike combing or graining. Think of the coloured glass marbles you played with as a child. The most common use for these papers in the last two hundred years has been for the endpapers, or flyleaves, of books.

However, two conservators-turned detectives at the County Record Office in Bow Lane have discovered that marbled papers were being made in Preston much earlier than was previously thought.

William Lambert was a printer and stationer in Preston, he made marbled paper in the town as early as 1679 - possibly earlier, using locally bought pigments and alum to produce the red, blue, white, yellow and green patterns which were in regular use here throughout the next hundred years. He died in 1688 and is buried in the parish church yard.

Researchers Mark Walmsley and Neil Sayer believe that Preston based Lambert possibly produced the first marbled paper in England at a date much earlier than the middle of the 18th century, previously though to be the operative date....**THE REST OF THE COUNTRY DOES TOMORROW.**

VIOLENCE IN VERSE

It was common in Victorian times for verses about tragedies to be written, printed and sold. Sometimes this was for a charitable purpose, but sometimes not, as in this Preston example. In earlier times, these printed sheets were called "*broadsides*". Preston was a major centre for the writing, printing and publishing of these ephemeral sheets.

VERSES WRITTEN TO LAMENT THE FEARFUL DEATH OF ANNIE
RATCLIFFE, who was murdered at Preston, by her lover,
John Aspinall Simpson on 3rd August, 1881

A sorrowful story I am going to tell
How a young girl in Preston by a murderer's hand fell,
Her sweetheart who vow'd to make her his wife,
First seduced the poor girl, and has now took her life.

This innocent girl Ann Ratcliffe by name,
From Darwen to Preston, some time ago came,
Beloved and respected she happy did dwell,
Along with her parents who kept the Blue Bell.

A young Preston clerk his addresses he paid,
And won the affections of that pretty maid,
They oft met together and as young lovers do,
He pledged his affections and vow'd to be true.

He'd seduced the poor girl it is plain to be seen
Tho' her age at the time had not reached sixteen,
She proved to be pregnant, and then he did say,
He'd make her his wife, and appointed the day.

The third day of August had been fixed upon,
When those two in wedlock were to be made one,
But he had no intention his vows to fulfil,
For on that very morning her blood he did spill.

She set out for St. Paul's in her wedding array,
And as she went out to her sister did say,
"I will not be long, when I'm married to John,
I'll come home and let you know how I got on".

She met her sweetheart, and quite free from alarms,
With him she went in the Sir Walter Scott Arms,
And in a short time as the facts do appear,
The girl's throat he severed from ear to ear.

In pools of her blood on the floor she did lie
While quite unconcerned her murderer sat by:
His hands stained with blood, and the razor also
While his motive for murder there's no one does know.

He must be a heartless and wicked young man,
To use such deception and form such a plan,
He brought the sharp razor on that fatal morn
To murder the girl and her baby unborn.

Her friends were distracted to hear she was dead,
And many a tear for her fate will be shed,
'Twas a terrible death for the poor girl to die,
But we hope she's at rest with the angels on high.

Verses written to lament the
FEARFUL DEATH
of
ANNIE RATCLIFFE,
Who was MURDERED at PRESTON, by her
lover, John Aspinall Simpson, on
AUGUST 3rd, 1881.

Another poem was written when
Simpson met Marwood, the public
hangman, in Manchester Prison in
November 1881.

MYLES PENNINGTON, WHARFINGER

Bob Dobson

It is the mark of a special man that, should he leave his home town for foreign fields and die there, he be fondly recalled by his former townsfolk.

Such a chap was Myles Pennington, who was born in 1814 at Lancaster where his father was agent for a carrier, by horse wagon and canal boat, called John Hargreaves. That man's name was as well known in freight circles as the famed one of Pickford. His high-speed (3 mph) flyboats carried goods but no passengers, on the *Lancaster Canal* between Kendal and Preston, thence by rail over the Ribble to join the *Leeds & Liverpool Canal* at Walton Summit. Young Myles was indoctrinated into the business of *"carrying"* even before he came to Preston as a teenager to be apprenticed to Hargreaves as a fly-boat office clerk.

He took an active part in the firm's business, but also found time to become heavily involved with the main men in the Temperance Movement. He had the zeal of a reformer in political, social and educational matters, *"a very earnest, practical, loyal man with a deep affection for those with whom he was associated in his early years"*.

The railway came to Preston when Myles was a young man, and he gained experience enough on the *"North Union"* goods side to be made the first goods manager of the new *"Preston & Wyre Railway"* when it opened in 1840. In his memoirs this period is recalled in some detail. He tells that the line was the first in England to make use of the electric telegraph, and that the celebratory dinner at Fleetwood Station to mark the opening was attended by George Stevenson. At Fleetwood, Myles teamed up with the then station agent, Henry Anderton, another Preston chap, who was *"the poet of the Temperance Movement"*.

Myles was responsible for increasing the revenue on the line by introducing cheap-day trips to the seaside. He had become so expert in the business of carrying goods that his former boss enticed him to Canada, where his skills in the managing of wharfs alongside the ocean, rivers, canals and railways were greatly valued. He continued to work into old age, loved and respected by all who came into contact with him because of his professional capabilities and feelings for his fellow men.

Myles wrote on the history of Temperance and an autobiography, "*Railways and Other Ways*". This was published in 1894, two years before he died in Canada. Preston was saddened by the death of this early apostle of temperance reform. He was a man of whom Preston can be proud.

* * * * * *

A CHILD LOST FOR FIVE YEARS:—The other night a widow named Roach, on her way from the North to Manchester, where she was expecting work as a seamstress, entered the tramp ward of the Preston Union Workhouse, at Fulwood. Next morning, previous to leaving the place, she chanced to say in the presence of a woman named Mansley and her children, who were also in the workhouse, that five years ago she lost at Preston a little girl named Mary Ann Roach. One of Mansley's children—a little girl—noticing the name, said that a playmate of her's at the workhouse often used to write her name down as "Mary Ann Roach," saying when doing so, that she had two names. Subsequently the porter at the workhouse made some inquiries, questioning the woman Roach and the girl separately. The way in which each of them referred to certain names and events agreed so markedly that there was no longer any doubt as to the girl being the daughter of the woman Roach; the latter was allowed to take charge of her, and they left the workhouse together. It seems that the girl was admitted to the house about five years ago, having been found in the streets. When admitted she was about eight years old, and at that time she gave her name as Nevil, that being her mother's maiden name. The girl had been taken out by a girl in Preston and lost. The mother, on recovering the child, stated that she had traversed the country for miles round in search of the child. On two or three occasions the woman, who is the widow of a soldier, has stayed for a short time at the Preston Workhouse, but owing to the child having given in the name of Nevil, she did not hear of her.

Not a social worker in sight; Imagine he trauma that 8years old Mary Ann went through when she realised her mother had left her. The Mother's anguish appears to have been much less, or she would have kept on looking for her lassie. Were the police notified? Who paid for the child's upkeep for those five years? Did they live happily ever after?

Here we have three examples of Preston businessmen – two of them trading from the same Fishergate premises a few years apart – using the Preston lamb on their invoices. Perhaps it was to give an impression of association with the Corporation or of their long-standing in the town, or of course they might have said it was to show their pride in Preston.

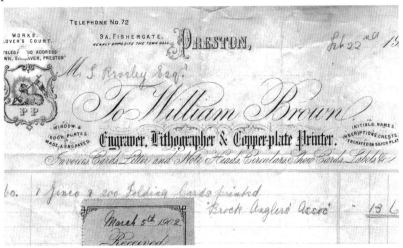

I suspect there are few, if any, of today's traders using the symbol in their notepaper.

Umbrellas and hats are no longer made in Preston, but a full century ago in Edwardian Preston they were, as evidenced by these adverts. Robert Coward spent a lot on advertising. He was also a gentlemen's hairdresser at premises in Friargate and Church Street. His father started the business in 1874 in Church Street and expanded into Friargate in 1868. They also sold walking sticks. Mr Burrows, who aligned his business with the Preston Lamb, started a shop in Lancaster Road in 1875, moving in 1878 to his spacious, double fronted, forty-eight feet wide with two large windows premises, which went back for about seventy five feet. No wonder he could carry a large stock of hats.

SOME CLOCKS AND BELLS IN PRESTON

Raymond Clayton

PRESTON TOWN HALL was opened on Thursday October 23rd 1867 by HRH the Duke of Cambridge.

The clock was by Potts of Leeds. There were four illuminated dials of 10ft. diameter. The bells were cast by John Taylor & Co. of Loughborough and were "*considered by campanologists to be excellent (the large bell especially) and with the exception of 'Big Ben' and 'Great Paul' or 'Mighty Tom' more powerful in effect than any in the Kingdom*".

	Dia	Weight	Note
1st quarter	2' 10"	9cwt 3qtr 3lbs	D sharp
2nd quarter	2' 11"	10cwt 3qtr 27lbs	C sharp
3rd quarter	3' 3"	12cwt 1qtr 10lbs	B sharp

This clock was destroyed in the fire of 15th March 1947.

When the previous Town Hall was demolished the clock was removed and still exists at Beech Grove Farm, Greenhalgh, Kirkham.

PRESTON PARISH CHURCH. The first record of bells appears in an inventory of 1552 "*iiij bells and fyft bell lent by Sir Ryc Houghton Knight*".

A peal of eight bells were cast in 1814 by Thomas Mears of London. In 1934, two more were added to make a peal of ten bells. At the same time, a new electric clock was installed with a unique set of quarter chimes composed by the vicar, Canon Wallis, with assistance from Mr Fuller-Maitland, music critic to *The Times.*

The present ring of bells consists of the eight bells from the redundant church of Holy Trinity, Bolton and two new bells. The two new trebles were the first Millennium bells cast at the Whitechapel Foundry, London.

Two more bells are to be installed making a ring of twelve. When the installation of the new bells is complete, work to restore the clock chimes will hopefully be taken in hand.

The following is taken from the *"Watch and Clock Maker"* for March 1935

"Electric Clock for Preston Parish Church"

The first electric turret clock in Preston, complete with striking and chiming gear, presented to Preston Parish Church by Mr and Mrs J R Goodwin, of Fulwood, is now in use. After 10 pm, the chimes and the striking are automatically silenced. The chimes were composed for a peal of 10 bells by Canon Wallis, Vicar of Preston. Smaller clocks have been fitted in various parts of the church and these, with the barrel clock, are under the control of a Pul-syn-etic master clock.

Mr J H Tonge of Preston was consulting engineer for the scheme and Messrs. Green & Son, Jewellers, Meadow Street, Preston, carried out the work under the personal supervision of Mr James Green".

Greens must have been proficient clock engineers as they also installed the master clock system in the present **Town Hall** and turret clocks at **Leyland, St Andrew and All Saints, Hesketh Bank.**

The largest bell in Preston is in the tower of **St Walburge's**. Cast by George Mears of London 1860, it weighs 31cwt.

A ring of six bells hung in the tower of **St Mark's** were scrapped in the 1960's. A chime of 10 hemispherical bells once hung in the tower of **St Luke's** church. These were installed to the memory of the dead of the First World War. These have recently been installed at **St Michael's**, Hoole.

Fishergate Baptist Church contains an electric turret clock installed in 1974. The original weight driven clock is in the Harris Museum.

The turret clock at **St Ignatius'** is an electric one.

The old **Harris Orphanage** contains a clock chiming the Cambridge quarters and has four dials of 5ft diameter installed 1887. There are four bells, the largest 20 ins. diameter.

Other clocks in the city include those in:-

The Civic Hostel (workhouse) : Former Park School : Christ Church (now in Lancashire County Council Building) : Fulwood Barracks
The Old Public Hall : Booth's Grocers Store, Fishergate
Former Preston Dock Offices.

SADDLER AND HARNESS MAKER

A. WATSON PRESCOTT

Established 1820

The Last Shop front in Preston

E. Beattie.

A WINDOW ON PRESTON

For many years, folks in Preston have been able to window shop before deciding whether to enter a shop to purchase. It wasn't always so, as plate glass only *"came in"* in the early 19th century. The date of Preston's first plate glass window isn't known, but the shop's owner is.

He was Richard Lawson, who came to Preston in 1832 as a fifteen years old Cockerham lad. He worked for his aunt for ten years before setting up as a hosier on his own account.

Knitted stockings were worn by gentlemen in those Georgian and early Victorian days, and he became known for high quality and *"perhaps the finest judge of hosiery in the kingdom"*.

His premises were in Cheapside and Fishergate, next door to the Town Hall. At the time of his death in 1903, he was *"the oldest hosier in England"*.

Richard's claim as to being the first to have plate glass windows needs looking into. It must refer to the size, as, at some time previous to 1810, John Beattie, a hairdresser, put up a shop front - see the illustration - which was then *"modern"* and is thought to have been the first such enhancement to a shop property in the old town. It was in Cheapside – it must have been close by Lawson's shop – and became occupied by Mr Watson, a saddler. It lasted until 1895 when, lamented by the *"Preston Guardian"*, its splendid frontage was sold for three shillings.

The opening of a new railway line to Fleetwood and Yorkshire was so important to Preston that the Mayor, John Paley and the Recorder, Mr Addison, dressed as navvies to cut the first sods and wheel them a considerable distance. Mr Pilkington of Bolton captured the scene for readers of the *"Illustrated London News"* in January 1847.

BUILDING SAINT WALBURGE'S

Tom Smith

Perhaps the most outstanding feature of Preston's skyline is the tower and spire of St. Walburge's church. The spire is the third highest in the country and rises to a height of over three hundred feet, making it a landmark for miles across the surrounding area. This most important graded building in the town was designed by Joseph Hansom and opened in 1854. He had already created a *'Patent Safety Cab'* some twenty years earlier and though he made little money out of this venture it later brought him fame and became one of the best known vehicles in the country. Hansom had settled in the town in 1847 when Preston was the centre of the most Catholic area in the country and its rapidly increasing population needed churches and schools. By 1850 it had 68,000 people, over a quarter of whom were Catholics with only four churches to accommodate them.

To cater for the expansion of the town on the western side it was decided to build boys' and girls' schools in Maudland. These schools were endowed by William Talbot, a local hosier and cotton manufacturer, and were designed by Hansom. Building them began in 1847 and when completed their wings provided two large classrooms. The entrance and cloakroom were used as a chapel whilst the intended church was being debated. The decision to build was finally taken in 1850 and the foundation stone was laid on Whit Monday of that year in the presence of over 8,000 people. Most of these had assembled in Winckley Square before marching across the town, banners aloft, flags flying and accompanied by several bands. In April 1853 the parish was formally separated from St. Wilfrid's but it was another sixteen months before the church was completed and opened.

The priests of the Society of Jesus, who took responsibility for the project, favoured the *'Decorated Gothic'* style of church building and chose Joseph Hansom because they had been pleased with his work on the Talbot Schools. Though achieving popular fame as the designer of the cab, during his professional life he was also the architect of fifty churches, ten convents and seven monasteries. Whilst the church was under construction his family lived at *'Canal Cottage'* on Tulketh Brow and later at *'Greenbank House'*. During this period both Joseph and his wife Hannah played a prominent part in fundraising activities, their eldest daughter, Sophie, was married in the school chapel in 1854. Her husband was George Maycock, a Prestonian, who later became famous as a designer of stained glass windows.

Built in mid-century, St. Walburge's ranks as one of the great churches of that period and is among Hansom's best. The internal breadth of the building was a hundred and sixty feet which was covered by a magnificent hammer beam roof, possibly inspired by that of the Great Palace Hall at Westminster. Each hammer beam was tipped by a standing figure of a saint, and the whole was a monumental piece of carpentry. Whilst this roof was in course of construction, a hurricane blew down three of the massive main timbers, each weighing six tons, and caused £200 worth of damage. Fortunately nobody was injured. Hansom's concept of such a wide single span roof was initially attacked and he strongly defended this design, claiming it had many precedents in medieval times. By 1872, however, it had become apparent that the weight of this roof which was unsupported by pillars was creating undue outward pressure against the walls. The church was considered by professionals to be seriously in danger of collapsing and the problem had to be remedied by strengthening the walls with buttresses.

One of Hansom's aims in church design was to improve the quality of accommodation, especially for the poor parishioners so that they could have a proper view of the altar. This he most certainly achieved at St. Walburge's. It is not, however, for its magnificent roof nor for its vast auditorium that it is famous. It is the tower and the spire on its southern side which attracts most attention. These were only added some years later in 1866 for their construction had been largely dictated by the pace at which money could be raised.

Industrial problems in Preston had led to extreme poverty among its working classes. From October 1854 to May 1855 *"the great lock-out"* took place when 25,000 cotton operatives were thrown out of work for seeking a pay restoration following an earlier reduction in wages. They eventually had to return defeated and dejected. Then, from 1861 to 1865 the American Civil War caused a *"Cotton Famine"* in Lancashire when most mill workers were unemployed and had to rely on food distributed by charity relief organisations. In December 1862, over 40,000 Prestonians were out of work and four months later forty mills were closed. The Maudland area in particular was badly affected, having the poorest and most neglected streets in the town. Church collections and building donations were naturally reduced.

The anticipated cost of the tower and spire was £4,630 and before the Cotton Famine only £650 had been raised. This was mainly the result, in September 1861, of a performance by amateurs at the Theatre Royal of Shakespeare's *"Hamlet"* and by a bazaar held the following month. The industrial situation gradually eased as supplies of raw cotton improved and from 1865 more efforts were made to raise the required capital. Joseph Hansom, who had left Preston in 1855 to work in Clifton, agreed to conduct the erection of the tower but within a short time he handed this over. The church itself had been made in brownish freestone but the tower and spire were to be made of limestone. There is a local tradition that because the area is sandy the foundations were laid on bales of cotton. This may well be correct for it would also have helped to reduce the vibration caused by the frequent passage of trains on the nearby railway lines.

It can be seen that the limestone blocks at the base of the tower to a height of about thirty feet look different from the rest. This is because they were originally used as sleepers on the Preston to Lancaster railway until they were replaced by wooden ones to make for a more comfortable ride. Such large limestone blocks going cheaply were a bargain the parish priest could not ignore. When Hansom retired from supervising the construction he was replaced by a Mr. Thomas from Wales who brought in a small amount of Welsh limestone but his business failed and he had to leave the task unfinished. The contract to complete the tower and spire was then undertaken by a local builder, Edward Bickerstaff, who used Kendal limestone, transported to Preston down the canal.

Progress remained slow because of lack of money and by October 1864 only a further twenty-eight feet had been added. Then in August 1865 a Tower and Spire Draw raised a further £1000 and this ensured that construction could begin again in earnest once the winter was over. Much of the building on the tower and spire was done therefore in the Spring and Summer of 1866 without a single accident taking place, despite the lofty height at which the work took place. Finally, in September 1866 the cross which surmounted the edifice was placed in position watched by a large crowd, many with binoculars and telescopes. The fixing of the lightning conductors a month later also attracted many spectators. Above the cross was put a weather vane made of copper and brass weighing 56lbs. This became known as the *'Maudland Cock'* and remained in position until 1931. It is now in the town museum. It was apparently a medieval papal enactment that the figure of a cock should be set on every church steeple as the emblem of St. Peter who thrice denied Jesus before the cock crowed.

The pinnacle was 408 feet above sea level and the highest point of the building was 311 feet 8 inches. The tower was 117 feet 6 inches, the spire 177 feet, 15 feet of ironwork on top and a weather vane of 2 feet 2 inches. There are only two higher spires in the country, those of Salisbury and Lichfield Cathedrals. After St. Paul's, London, it is the tallest church.

By 1881, however, the spire and tower were causing concern and a survey revealed defects in the ironwork. Pointing was needed and some of the stonework which was perishing and cracking needed replacement. It was also found that the interior spaces had been carelessly filled with rubble and concrete had to be poured in to form a solid base on which the spire rested. Similar problems occurred again in 1923 and there remains the need for regular supervision and thorough checks to ensure that St. Walburge's does not deteriorate beyond repair. Whilst we should be proud of the architectural achievements of our forefathers we have also to be very much aware of the legacy of preservation and its cost which they have bequeathed to us.

It is possible to ascend the tower, though few visiting parties have been arranged in recent years. This is because of essential and ongoing restoration work. Anyone particularly interested in such a visit should contact the parish priest, Fr. Peter Sayer, Tel .01772 726370.

WHIT WALKS

Much of the history of Preston revolves around its churches and chapels – Roman Catholic, Anglican and Non-Conformist. In the 1840's a tradition was started which was to last almost a hundred years – that of holding processions of witness on Whit Monday. The numbers taking part was a spectacle in itself. Here is what the *Manchester Guardian* told its readers in 1878. It is interesting to see that it was a holiday as well as a holy day, and that the great industrial dispute of that year did not totally prevent folk from doing what they always did on Whit Monday:-

WHIT MONDAY AT PRESTON

"Notwithstanding the threatening aspect of the weather in the early morning the sun broke out about ten o'clock, and the remainder of the day, though cloudy at times, was very favourable for the usual processions. The Roman Catholic guilds mustered in Winckley Square at ten o'clock. The procession was composed as follows:- St. Ignatius's Guild, 800; Church of the English Martyres, 580; St. Wilfred's; 470, St. Augustine's, 870; St. Walburge's, 600; St. Joseph's, 330; total, 3,650. Each section of the guilds was headed by the pastors of the church to which they belonged, and two or three bands accompanied it. This procession occupied 50 minutes in passing a given point. The Church of England schools started in procession from Church-street, opposite the Parish Church, at 2.15 p.m. in the following order, and went round Winckley Square and through the principal thoroughfares, headed each by a band and their respective clergy and superintendents:- Parish Church Schools, 500; Trinity, 240; St. Mary's, 2,000; St. Peter's, 950; St. Paul's, 1,100; Christ Church, 826; St. Thomas's, 880; St. James's, 270; All Saint's, 900; St. Luke's, 550; St. Mark's, 828; Emmanuel's, 600; and St. Saviour's, 1,100; total 10,834. This procession occupied an hour and 20 minutes in passing any one point, but there were some lengthy gaps between the schools. The Market Place and the Orchard were as full as usual of hobby horses, shows, and swings, and though they seemed to be doing a good business in spite of the lock-out, money was not so plentiful in the fair as on former Whit-Mondays".

DRY AS A BADGER.

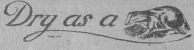
98

THE PRESTON BOROUGH POLICE FORCE
- THE EARLY YEARS

Shane Byrne

Before an established police force was present in Preston, the streets were patrolled at night by a watch, comprised of elderly volunteers who received little in a way of compensation for their long hours. The borough council's *Improvement Commission* established the *Preston Municipal Police Force* officially in 1815. It created a police force of seven officers. Three councillors were appointed Police Commissioners to regulate the force. Thomas Walton, a reedmaker, was appointed the first superintendent, and he was assisted by an inspector and five constables. His pay was based on performance; the more people convicted, the more pay he received.

In 1835 the government passed the *Municipal Corporations Act*. This reorganised large borough authorities and saw an increase in the franchise eligible to vote. One of the sections of the Act required the council to appoint a *Watch Committee* to oversee the administration of a police force within the district. The first meeting of the Preston Watch Committee was held on January 1st 1836 at the Town Hall. At this meeting seven men were appointed to the Watch Committee:- Thomas Miller, (the Mayor), Alderman Haydock, Alderman Monk, and Messrs. Leach, Livesey, Walker and Holmes. The Committee appointed Samuel Banister as the new superintendent of the force, and augmented it to ten officers.

The force was first stationed in the Turks Head Yard area. However, in 1832 it moved to a new police station on Avenham Street, just off Fishergate. This wasn't the only police presence in the town. During the 1830s and 1840s men were stationed in the Moor Lane area in lodging houses at either end of the road. Men were also stationed in the Deepdale area. These men had their rent, gas and water paid for by the Watch Committee. In 1858 the Police force moved to a new facility on Lancaster Road, a station that cost £6013 18s 11d to build and included the Police Court. (now called the Magistrate's Court).

The structure and size of the Preston Borough Police Force altered considerably throughout the nineteenth century. Up until 1836 the force had been around seven men, each man having to work twelve hours shifts, either day or night. In 1836 the hours worked were similar but with a slightly larger body of men, around ten to fifteen officers, until the mid-1840s. It was in this decade that a hierarchical structure was established. Below the superintendent was an inspector, two sergeants and twelve constabulary. The wage structure was altered to reflect this establish the hierarchy. The inspector received twenty-eight shillings, the sergeants a guinea, and the constables seventeen shillings each per week. The structure and strength of the force remained in place until 1847 when it was augmented to twenty-two men and a detective branch was established from the day duty officers. These detectives were paid more than the other constables. This hierarchical structure was further enhanced by the subdivision of the constable rank into four classes.:- merit class, 1st class, 2nd class and 3rd class, and again the wage structure reflected the position within the hierarchy. The hierarchy was established to reward those officers who remained in their positions for longer than two years. The force was augmented in the 1850s to sixty constables, with further increases throughout the 1860s, 1870s and 1880s until the force stood at ninety-five men in 1882.

The occupational background of the recruits to the force was quite diverse. Men from all kinds of trades became policemen during this period: from blacksmiths to soldiers, from sailors to platelayers. However, the majority of recruits were made up of labourers, either agricultural migrants from the Fylde area or workers in warehouses within Preston. Some two hundred applicants stated that they were labourers. The next largest supplier of recruits was the cotton industry that dominated Preston throughout the nineteenth century. Spinners, weavers, dyers, clothmakers and many other who were involved in the industry in some way found their way into the force. This could be explained by cyclic downturns in the fortunes of the industry, as policing was a lower paid job than the cotton workers would earn.

A Preston police officer's uniform did not alter much over the time of study. In 1832 a new uniform was ordered based upon the style of the *Metropolitan Police,* formed in 1829. The uniform consisted of a suit of blue cloth, a frock coat, a wide leather belt, and a chimney pot hat with a letter P on it to represent Police. *(though it possible that it stood for Preston).* In 1836, the Watch Committee issued uniforms to the officers free of charge, however the officers were responsible for its upkeep and were to wear the uniform at all times, especially during Sunday services. This uniform consisted of a coat, a pair of trousers, *soon increased to two pairs,* a topcoat, a hat, a cape, two pairs of Blucher boots, handcuffs and a truncheon. Night duty officers were each given a lantern to aid them on their beats. A subsidy was usually given for the upkeep of the boots, as these were more likely to be worn out by the long hours of walking. Brass plates were added to the uniform during the latter months of 1836, but it wasn't until the 1840s that policemen were given numbers worn on their collars for recognition.

A policeman's life was a hard one. At the beginning of this period the officers were working twelve hours shifts, either day or night. In 1836 the Watch Committee gave four officers day duty, which involved working from 9am until midnight. The night shift was divided into two sections, four officers patrolled from 7pm to 7am, and the other two from 9am to 9pm.This time scale altered very little throughout this period. As the force grew, so did the number of beats and the times of duty altered slightly. In April 1847 five men were ordered to work from 1pm to midnight, four men were to work from midnight-4am, and several others were to work from midnight to 9am. Beats usually involved several streets that had to be patrolled throughout the time they were on duty. Officers were given no holiday time until 1847, when they were granted one day's leave every fortnight. It was not until 1868 that the Watch Committee allowed officers a week's holiday between the period of April and October. Long hours were not the only thing hazardous to an officer. On several occasions   discontented persons assaulted officers. One such event in July 1839 saw officers Rigby, Curle and Leach seriously injured. Investigating a disturbance between several Irish navvies at a local public house the three men were set upon by a large number of them. Leach suffered broken ribs, Curle a gashed head and Rigby was off work for two weeks with his injuries.

A policeman's life was not made easier by the harsh discipline.The   disciplinary system was used by the Watch Committee to punish those officers who broke the code of conduct laid down. Usually for a first offence an officer was summoned in front of the Committee to answer the charge against him. After this the officer would be reprimanded and warned about his future conduct. The second form was to impose a fine upon the officer ranging from five shillings to an entire week or two weeks wages. These were usually levied for more serious offences, or on repeat offenders. Another method incorporated by the Watch Committee was suspension, usually imposed upon officers who had committed severe offences. The most severe form of punishment was *dismissal*. This was extremely frequent during the early decades of the force. Usually reserved for those officers who the Watch Committee believed were inappropriate or unfit to continue as policemen, men who had been called before the Committee on several occasions, or simply for a major breach of the disciplinary system. The majority of men dismissed in the early decades were men caught drinking. Policemen succumbed in large numbers to the temptations of liquor. Police officers Edward Worthington and William Gordon were finally dismissed after both being caught four times drinking on duty. The Watch Committee loathed persistent drinkers, and throughout this time men like Worthington and Gordon did not last long as officers if they were susceptible to the lure of alcohol.

* * * * * *

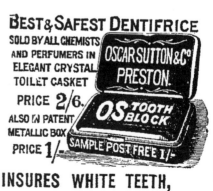

The Preston Borough Police Force was founded in 1815, twenty four years before the Lancashire Constabulary. The forces were amalgamated on 1st April 1969. Here we see the traffic patrol section of the Borough Force awaiting inspection by Her Majesty's Inspector in 1949. This was a means of ensuring that a force maintained its efficiency. The Chief Constable, Mr Garth, would be pointing out the fine motor cars, motor bikes and well-maintained bicycles which used to patrol the town. The vehicles' registration numbers all include the letters RN or CK, which were the two sets of letters issued to the Borough Council.

R. SLINGER & SON,

Range Manufacturers,

FURNISHING and
BUILDERS' IRONMONGERS,
MILL FURNISHERS,

Friargate and Corporation Street,

PRESTON.

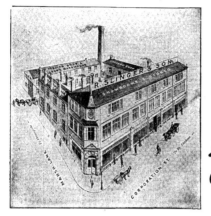

Telephones : 12 and 171 (two lines) connecting all Departments.   Telegrams : "Slinger, Preston."

There are very few businesses trading in Preston today which were trading when Victoria reigned. Slinger's is one them. They were founded in 1858, a fact referred to in their website address, and occupied premises in Friargate in 1875. Two years later their wood-cutting machines won them a sliver medal, proudly shown on their letter-heading, at the Preston Agricultural Society's meeting. The company is in the hands of the Slinger family still, and operates from Paley Road. This invoice is dated 1903. Five years later, when the advert appeared they had acquired a telephone line.

Closed on Thursdays at 1 o'clock.   TELEGRAMS—"Slinger, Ironmonger, Preston."
TELEPHONE No. 12.

WORKS & WAREHOUSE
CORPORATION ST.

........, Friargate, Preston, ... 190...

To R. Slinger & Son,

SAW MAKERS, GENERAL IRONMONGERS & MACHINISTS.

CIRCULAR SAW BENCHES, BAND SEWING MACHINES, PLANING AND MOULDING MACHINES, DRILLING MACHINES, ANVILS, VICES, TUE IRONS, PATENT MAIL AXLES, CART ARMS, PATENT POINTED HORSE NAILS, &C., &C.

Folio............Dept.........   **Kitchen Fire Ranges, Marble and Slate Chimney Pieces.**

PUBLIC HEALTH IN PRESTON BEFORE 1850

Tom Smith

One of the greatest social needs in this country during the 19th century was the improvement of public health. Keeping the area around your own property clean had long been regarded as the duty of the individual and had failed abysmally. Only gradually during Victorian times did it become recognised as the responsibility of the community. Drainage, sanitation, refuse removal, the state of houses, streets and roads, and the quality of the water supply were eventually seen by local councils as their obligation. This, however, was only slowly forced upon them by the appalling death rates which resulted from poor housing, inadequate sewerage, unpaved streets, bad drainage, the dangers of shallow, overcrowded graveyards in town centres and polluted water supplies. Preston was as bad as any town in the country.

During the 18th century Preston had been a social centre attracting aristocratic and leading families to its annual season. Accounts of the town by Celia Fiennes, Daniel Defoe and Lady Oxford described its fine houses, wide streets and bracing air. The assemblies, theatres, races, Guild festivities and the attractions of Avenham Walks together with improvements in house building and street lighting were all indications of its progress. Yet these did not give a true picture of the town as a whole. A study of the records of the Preston Court Leet reveals the problems caused by the *"common nuisance"* which would appal to-day's citizens who complain about the litter in the streets.

Before the Industrial Age, most of the difficulties were caused by middens and dunghills in the streets and behind houses or disposed of on any waste ground inside or outside the town. Garbage, ashes, household refuse and urine were thrown on the pavements or swept into the nearest gutter or channel running down the middle of the street which only cleared when it rained heavily. Pigs were allowed to scavenge anywhere, drinking wells were often fouled and dead animals left to rot in wayside ditches. The thirty or so butchers whose shops were in the town's Shambles were regularly fined for slaughtering cattle, sheep and poultry outside their premises, throwing the guts and garbage into the street and leaving it there. The few public scavengers could neither keep on top of their task nor satisfactorily dispose of their unwholesome collections. The smell which hung around the town must have been dreadful. Our ancestors were apparently content to wallow in their own filth.

The first spinning mill had been opened in the town in 1777 and more factories were built from the 1790s onwards. When the first national census was taken in 1801 the population of Preston was 11,887 and fifty years later it had grown to 69,450. From what had been described as *"one of the prettiest retirements in England"* in 1758 a century later had become a typically dirty, smoky cotton town and parts of it were among the worst in England. Migrant workers who moved in seeking employment often brought with them the primitive sanitary standards of the countryside

A survey for the *'Health of Towns Commission'* was made of Preston in 1841 by Rev. John Clay, the chaplain at the local House of Correction, and another was undertaken eight years later by George T. Clark, inspector of the General Board of Health. It is their reports which provide us with the horrendous account of the dreadful conditions which the inhabitants of the unplanned and rapidly expanding town had to endure.

The drainage system was hardly a system at all. Sewers were made of rough stone without being set in mortar and were usually much too shallow to allow the many cellar dwellings to drain into them. Refuse and litter accumulated in large open middens and those houses which had private privies tended to be linked to the nearest cesspits by gutters which drained across the footpaths and frequently overflowed. Lack of scavenging regularly caused animal and vegetable refuse to pour onto the middle of the pavement, if indeed it was actually paved. Around Bolton's Court, off Stoneygate, was *"a range of piggeries and dung heaps with a large trough for the storage and mixing of manure".* At the bottom of Lune Street was a huge cesspit which naturally filled with water, especially after heavy rain, collecting it from both sides of Friargate and what is now the Ring Road. The nearby brows were much steeper than nowadays because they have all been lowered at various times in the last two hundred years to assist the progress of traffic.

Another cause of distress in the 1820s was the inadequate provision of water. A water supply had been installed in 1729 at the bottom of Avenham Street and Main Sprit Weind and was pumped around the town in 2,500 yards of wooden pipes. There were also fifteen public draw wells which were used until 1822. As the town expanded this supply proved to be far too irregular, inadequate, unfiltered and contaminated. In 1832 the Preston Water Works Company was formed and supplies gradually began to improve. It was amazing that during the national cholera epidemic of 1831-1832 there were only ten cases in Preston and only five of these died. Few houses had running water so there was a lack of personal cleanliness and clean clothing especially among the poorest people. Many lived in dirty, crowded rooms where there was an almost complete absence of fresh air and in which whole families lived, cooked, ate and slept.

It was little wonder that the average height of lower class townspeople in Lancashire, according to Dr. Gaskell writing in 1836, was only five feet six inches, their limbs slender and ungainly, their legs often bowed and their hair thin and straight. Dysentery, fever, bronchitis, typhus, influenza, whooping cough, measles, scarlet fever and smallpox were all commonplace and not only badly affected many children but could wipe out whole families. In Preston in 1848 the expectancy of life for the poorer classes was 18.23 years, for tradesmen 31.63 years, and for gentry 47.39 years. By mid-century the worst hit were invariably the immigrants from Ireland and typhus became known as *"Irish Fever"*. Equally dreadful was the high rate of infant mortality, as was the number of deaths among young mothers who had too many children too frequently in the most unclinical conditions.

Unfortunately medical facilities were scarce as practitioners and qualified doctors were almost non-existent. In 1825 there were only three physicians, fifteen surgeons and eight druggists in the whole of Preston and none were listed with qualifications in the town's directory. Their treatment of the sick would mainly involve leaching, saline injections, tobacco enemas for chest complaints, mercury and opium emetics for digestive disorders, and laudanum for restless children. No wonder that the mortality of children whose parents could afford to be in *'sick clubs'* and have them medically treated was as high as the others.

Most diseases could be dealt with at the Dispensary which had been established in Fishergate in 1809 and at the House of Recovery built in 1833. Here all expenses for patients and doctors were raised by local charities and endowments and they did fine work, for by 1849 they claimed that 3,618 people had been treated. Even there the standard could not have been high. One matron was Elizabeth Holden who was paid £20 a year but she was described as incompetent and unskilled and in 1846 was dismissed for drunkenness.

Over the years, several attempts by the Corporation had been made to improve matters though with little success. In 1815 the Preston Improvement Act removed the task of *"preventing common nuisances"* and supervising scavenging from the almost defunct Court Leet. In 1821 the flagging of town centre pavements was begun. Unfortunately the population and the erection of bad housing by unscrupulous landlords continued to increase. Before the reform of local government in 1835, the town council had little power to make positive improvements even if it could afford them.

In 1848 Parliament introduced a Public Health Act which placed responsibility for the basic requirements of public health and hygiene on borough councils. Towns were obliged to set up a Board of Health if more than 10% of the inhabitants petitioned or if the local death rate was over 2.3 per thousand. Preston easily fell into this second category and a board was established in 1850. One of its first measures was to arrange for a new public cemetery on the outskirts in Ribbleton and another was to appoint an inspector of nuisances. The town reservoir at Grimsargh was improved, more streets were paved and a public bath was opened. Other ongoing tasks included improving the town's sewerage system, removing stagnant water, demolishing pig sties, providing water closets, and appointing twenty-four scavengers to try to remove the rubbish, filth, middens and cesspools.

This was indeed progress but how successful or how many problems were actually solved is difficult to assess. In the twenty years between 1880 and 1900, Preston had the highest rate of infant mortality in the country on fifteen occasions and was second three times. Proud Preston was certainly not a good place to live, especially if you were poor.

PRESTON'S SOILED REPUTATION

In 1851, a Mr Binns produced *"Notes on the Agriculture of Lancashire"*. He had this to say about Preston .....

"Around the manufacturing town of Preston much of the land is of a strong tenacious character, and when drained is tolerably fertile. The soil is about twelve inches in depth, with a large admixture of clay, underneath which lies a hard solid mass of brick clay, and below that again a bed of mark, which from its admixture of clay is more adapted for lighter soils than for those already too adhesive. These strong clay lands are found generally in the higher level of the country. On the lower levels, both marsh and moss land afford a variety to the operations of the husbandman.

The march or alluvial soils are some of the richest in the country, particularly on the borders of the Ribble: at Lytham there is much of this alluvial soil, which also extends considerably inland. Near a large manufacturing town, where the great demand for milk and butter requires that a great extent of land should be devoted to their production, the prevailing opinion is, that this should be accomplished by natural grass; this, however, is by no means essential, as the artificial grasses, such as clover, Italian rye grass, and vetches, will afford more nutriment than any common pasture can possibly do, and as the quantity of milk given depends on the nutritious quality of the food, and the mode in which it is acquired, such grasses are well calculated for the dairy. From this kind of food the butter and cheese may not be quite equal in quality to that made from old pastures, but the deficiency in quality is more than compensated by an increase of quantity. At no great distance from the town where mixed husbandry is observed, the proportion of arable land to that in grass is about one-fourth, but this proportion increases as a better knowledge of the alternate and green crop husbandry becomes evident. There is perhaps no district in the kingdom which exhibits to the traveller such a succession of execrable old blue pastures as for miles to the south of Preston The land has been marled and ploughed till it could grow corn no longer, then left in its stiff, undrained, and exhausted state, to the efforts of nature, without any seeds being sown; that these fields should remain in this scandalous and unprofitable condition reflects great discredit upon both landlord and tenant. The old system of growing two or more grain crops in succession, as well as that of sowing beans broadcast, often with a mixture of peas or tares, by which the land becomes very weedy, and a naked fallow becomes indispensable, are now nearly abandoned. It is very clear that in the strong clay soils, such as prevail in this vicinity, no system of arable culture can be profitably carried on until draining is thoroughly effected; and I am glad to say that many of tile manufactories have lately been erected in the district, and are in full employ

The late Colonel Rawsthorne used one of Messrs. Garrett's drill machines, for grain crops; some of his wheat was drilled at fourteen inches apart and some at nine inches. The saving of seed he considered great, as in one instance, there were only six pecks sown to the acre – in the other only four, and yet the wheat was too thick on the ground".

* * * * * *

LET THERE BE LIGHT

Bob Dobson

In 1902, the Preston Town Clerk, Mr Hamer, responded to a circular letter sent out by his counterpart in Blackburn. It is likely that this was because Blackburn were going to appoint a new Lamp Superintendent, and wanted to know what his responsibilities would be and how much he should be paid. It gives us a glimpse into a dimly-lit corner of Preston's past.

Preston's population was then 112,982 and covered 4030 acres. The Lamp Superintendent was also *"Inspector of Gas Meters"* and was paid £2 a week. He was not provided with a uniform and there was no printed definition of his duties. He had charge of both gas and electric lamps. He did not receive a pass allowing free tram travel, nor did he get a bicycle provided. He had 28 men to supervise, and they looked after a total of 2907 gas lamps (2422 ordinary, and 485 incandescent), as well as 42 electric arc lamps (but no incandescent ones).

A HISTORY OF NATURAL HISTORY ASSOCIATIONS IN PRESTON

by Stephen R. Halliwell

For nearly two hundred years the mystery of the natural world which surrounds us has prompted Preston folk to come together to investigate and enjoy it. From relatively short-lived botanical societies to the long-running Preston Scientific Society, which is *"not-out"* after 110 years. There was a proliferation of this type of society during the last quarter of the 19th century in the major British conurbations.

Earliest traces refer to two Botanical Societies, the one formed in 1804 was still in existence in 1821 and meeting at the *'Green Man'* in Lord Street. At its formation in 1804 meetings were held at the *'Butcher's Arms'* in Molyneux Square, a thoroughfare into which Lord Street ran. During the lifetime of that society an off-shoot was formed, meeting at the *'Lamb and Packet'* in Friargate. It was said of the latter organization that *"they possessed books upon the science (of botany), and are assiduous in exploring the neighbourhood for plants".* The word *'plant'* incidentally, had a rather broader meaning than it has now: in fact in the years leading to the formation of these societies, anything living that didn't move was a *'plant'.* A person who studied *'plants'* was a botanist!

As the years passed there were further Botanical Societies, Naturalist Field Clubs and Natural History Societies, which appear to have concentrated mainly on botany. A report in the *'Preston Chronicle'* in 1867 tells of a field trip made by the Preston Field Naturalists to Red Scar, finding Marsh Gentians *(Gentiana pneumonanthe),* a species which is long extinct in the area. Further evidence pointing towards a botanical bias can be seen at the time a Preston Natural History Society was formed in 1824.

Periodically, throughout the nineteenth century associations such as Literary andPhilosophical Societies, or Institutes for the Diffusion of Useful Knowledge (more commonly known as Mechanics' Institutes) were established. In fact, Moses Holden was one of the principal promoters of the Literary and Philosophical ideal in Preston in the 19th century. Both of these organizations had a section of their membership who had an interest in natural history. The demise of the societies was often blamed on apathy but it was never always clear with whom the apathy lay, the leaders or the led.

The fore-runner of the present long-running society; an identically named Preston Scientific Society was formed in 1876 and initially had around one hundred members, but after a duration of only four years it came to a rather abrupt end. The only apparent reason that was given to the membership of 115 was that *"there were only two lectures booked for the approaching Winter Season"*.

Regardless, another attempt was made in 1893 to re-establish a Scientific Society in the town, learning hopefully from past mistakes. The prime movers in the creation of the 1893 Society were, as was usually the case in this type of association, leading local dignitaries, members of the legal and medical professions, and the clergy. About half of them had been involved in the failed 1876 Society. This time, however, no expense was spared in giving the new society the best possible chance of survival, with a huge launch held in the form of a fund-raising exhibition, known as a *'Conversazione'.* It was a huge success. So successful was the new-born society that by 1900 there were about 700 members, meetings were held five nights a week to cater for the variety of interest groups which flourished under the umbrella of the mother-society. One such group was the Microscopical and Natural History Section, in which no doubt the current Natural History Society has its roots. It would seem from the evidence that the principal natural history attraction was still botany, although at a time when F.S. Mitchell's *"Birds of Lancashire"* had just been published, one would think that there must have been some local ornithological interest. However, it was the botanists' *"endeavours and careful recording"* that resulted in the publication of *"The Flora of Preston and District"* around the turn of the century. The *'Flora'* was the product of a combined effort of nine of the members, under the leadership of the chairman, William Clitheroe.

Other sections within the society, each meeting on a different night of the week, were a Literary group, an Art Group and a Physical Science Group. There was something for everybody, and this remained constant until the early 1970's.

Many of the first 35 years of the society's existence were spent in premises in Fishergate close to Cheapside, before moving in 1929 to the Ellesmere Chambers in Church Street, and it was during the early days there that there was the first perceived instability. That was in 1904 when E.H. Turner, the then President, moved away from the town. In retrospect the event was probably viewed out of all proportion, but a stoical attitude was adopted, nevertheless, along the lines of the Lancashire dialect expression *"When one doore shuts another allus oppens";* and *'oppen'* it did, when George Joseph Gibbs moved into the town and joined the society. Gibbs was a Civil Engineer with a passion for astronomy - the present observatory on Moor Park was designed by him, and equipped on his advice, although it is his distant predecessor whose memory is commemorated in the *"Jeremiah Horrocks Observatory".* Gibbs later became the Honorary Curator of it. His love of all things cultural, his enthusiasm and encouragement, all contributed to him becoming something of a bed-rock for the society. In addition to taking an active role in the running of the Society, he gave many lectures to its members, mainly on astronomy.

He died at the age of 80 in the 1940's, but even today he is spoken of in terms that would be appropriate if he was known to us. His daughter, Winifred M. Gibbs, was associated with the society for a further 25 years, the last five of which she was the president.

Another group, this time with a lifespan of about 45 years from its inception in the late 1930's was the *"Record and Survey Committee".* The committee, which worked very closely with its much longer running sister group, the Photographic Section, had as their objective the recording of Preston as it was then, in mainly photographic form, at a time when so many changes in the town were anticipated; changesthat were to alter the appearance of much of the town forever. The results of their work, spreading to many volumes, can be seen and enjoyed in the Preston Reference Library where they are held for safe-keeping. The photographs collected now total about seven hundred, and though obviously unique to the town could also be unique as a collection, for it is believed that few other towns or boroughs has such a thorough record of the changes that have occurred.

The committee, never exceeding about nine, including three co-opted from the

Photographic Section, met monthly for many years to discuss opportunities as they presented themselves. In the later years this was reduced to bi-monthly, not because of any loss of interest, but as time passed most of the changes had been effected and the opportunities reduced. For many years they maintained a working relationship with the Borough Surveyor who kept them informed of impending changes.

In the early 1980's the tenancy of the Ellesmere Chambers, Church Street, came to an end after a period of more than 50 years, and a move was unavoidable. The following 15 years or so saw the society move a number of times each winter as *'developers'* rendered their home no longer suitable. The society by this time had also lost its Photographic and Record & Survey Committee partners - the former branching out on its own, and the latter becoming a 'sleeping-partner' capable of being revived if the need arose - becoming the society it resembles today. It was around this time that the word *'Scientific'* was deemed to have become somewhat outdated and, following many debates, eventually dropped, leaving *'The Preston Society'* as its title. In an attempt to convey what the society represents, the words *'Bird-watching and Natural History'* are used in conjunction with the official name. The society has always regarded the town centre as its home and efforts were made to keep it so, but in 2001 it was found necessary to move to the current meeting place in St. Mary's Church Hall, Cop Lane, Penwortham.

The current membership of around forty are, in the main, ornithologists who continue to meet each Monday evening during the winter months, enjoying over 20 lectures on a wide range of natural history topics, given in many instances by the leading members of their particular interest.

The spring and summer months see members meeting on Monday evenings to enjoy walks in various parts of the outlying district, in much the same way as their *"field naturalist"* and *"botanical"* predecessors did some 200 years ago

CLUBBING ON SATURDAY NIGHT

On a Saturday night in Preston there'll be *"youngsters"* going to a night club and those slightly older going to a club which might be of a working men's or social variety. Preston printer, publisher and historian William Dobson remembered a different sort of way to spend a Saturday evening in the late 1700's. He wrote ....

"Towards the close of the last century there was in Preston a "Saturday Night Club", which was attended by the tradesmen and shopkeepers of the town, who met together to enjoy their pipe and glass, and talk over the news. It was the custom at each meeting to appoint, in turns, one of the members to look out during the ensuing week for the house at which the best ale was sold. The club was next to be held there, and it was the duty of the ale-tasters for the time being, when he had obtained the important information, to write the name of the inn on a slate hung behind the door of the shop at the corner of Fishergate and Cheapside, kept by Mrs Alsop, a relative, and the predecessor in business, of the late Mr. Leach, hosier. I have been told by an old tradesman that he was often sent, when an apprentice, to look at the slates, in order to ascertain, for his master, where the club would meet. About the same time, there was also a club of the more aristocratic inhabitants, and this met more frequently: indeed, I believe, every night. This club varied its headquarters according to the quality of the ale, and the same course was taken to obtain information as to where the best ale was sold; but the shop where the slate was hung for the "Old Chums", as this club was called, was the one kept by Mr William Wilson, draper, in the Old Shambles. An old gentleman informs me that he was often, when a boy, asked by alderman, a member of the club, to 'run to Billy Wilson's, to see where the 'Old Chums' meet to-night.

I have lately come into possession of a card containing a printed list of the names of "The members of the Old Saturday Night Club" which is as follows:- Messrs. Wm. Brade, Tho. Crane, Rob. Ablatt, Rich. Walton, Rich. Baines, John Alsop, Tho. Russell, Wm. Collison, John Watson, senr., Sam. Crane, Wm. Carr, Wm. Bowran, John Ainsworth, Miles Forrest, Tho. Myers, Rob. Leach, Hen. Fisher. Possibly some old townspeople may recognise in the names some ancient family of whom they know nothing".

Wm. Dobson

STATISTIC NUMBER ONE

Agnes Hutchinson, an 88 years old widow from Canute Street, has a place in Preston's history. On Monday 15th August, 1904, she was knocked down by a tram, receiving a head injury from which she died a few days later. She was the first such fatality.

William Hindle was driving "No. 19" near the Co-op Stores in Lancaster Road about 5 o'clock. He stopped to pick up some passengers .... *"there was a lurry in my path and another lurry approaching on the next set of rails. I was constantly ringing my bell to clear the line when the lady stepped immediately in front of me. I applied the electric brake and pulled up immediately, but she had fallen onto the lifeguard, which came into operation"*

Mrs Hutchinson had a cap and shawl over her head, so perhaps she hadn't heard the bell clanging. The inquest jury returned a verdict of *"Accidental Death"* and exonerated the driver.

* * * * * *

The numbering of houses in Preston's streets was made compulsory in June 1851 when the Corporation passed a resolution under the authority Public Health Act to comple all householders to number their houses. This was because of the many streets in which less than half of the doors had no number displayed.

THE EARLY YEARS OF "THE PRESTON INSTITUTE FOR THE DIFFUSION OF KNOWLEDGE"

Tom Smith

In 2003 the University of Central Lancashire in Preston will celebrate the 175th anniversary of the founding of the Institution from which it traces its direct descent. None of the men involved in this venture in 1828 could ever have dreamed that one day it would flourish so abundantly as to become a university with over 24,000 full-time and part-time students. It is now one of the largest in the country and attracts people from all over the world. Yet the formative years of the Institution were a continuous struggle for existence let alone for progress and few of the early members could have faced the future with genuine confidence in its survival.

The first textile factory was opened in Preston in 1777 but it was not until John Horrocks settled in the town and opened his '*Yellow Mill*' in 1791 that more were built. Cotton manufacturing was a relatively new industry in which the system of apprenticeship for training youths did not exist. Yet for such as millwrights, machine-makers, foremen and mill managers there developed a need for knowledge of the scientific and technical principles underlying many of the mechanical operations in the factories. The lack of training for these men was appreciated by Dr. George Birkbeck, Leonard Horner and Lord Henry Brougham who were credited with starting a national movement for institutions which provided lectures, classes and libraries where they could learn the rudiments of science and mechanics. Consequently these became known as '*Mechanics' Institutes*' and they became widespread during the 1820s. By 1826 they existed in seven Lancashire towns and two years later one was opened in Preston.

Preston was one of the oldest chartered boroughs in the country and had been the focus of the county's social life in the 18th century as well as its administrative and judicial centre. It was not a typical Lancashire cotton town, though like most textile centres it had expanded rapidly from 11,887 in 1801 to 33,122 by 1831. Nevertheless it did not lack adult educational facilities. A valuable library was bequeathed to the town by Dr. Richard Shepherd who had been Mayor in 1747 and

1755. A '*Literary and Philosophical Society*' was formed in 1810 but only existed for six years. Night school classes on the Town Hall premises were unsuccessfully proposed in 1814 and 1817 and another had a brief existence until 1818 which was attended by "*fifty poor men and a few older apprentices*" A Catholic school opened in Fox Street in 1814 provided evening classes for adults in elementary subjects and a similar venture was supported in Shepherd Street by Joseph Livesey. He started a Sunday school in 1828 for educating young men. He also provided reading rooms in Shepherd Street and Market Street for working men, though these tended to be clerks and shopkeepers rather than tradesmen and factory hands.

On 23rd August 1828 a letter in the '*Preston Chronicle*' advocated the establishment of an adult educational institution, sarcastically referring to Preston being the last in the field as usual for such movements. Signed "*L*", it was probably written by Joseph Livesey and it invited prominent townsmen to a meeting in Mr. Smith's Rooms at No.11 Cannon Street. Twenty-four attended and supported the resolution. At a further meeting held on 7th October at the Corn Exchange under the chairman Dr. John Gilbertson , rules were adopted and officers were appointed. They decided against using the term "*Mechanic's Institute*" because it was not only for such workers that it was being formed.

The first officers of the '*Preston Institution for the Diffusion of Knowledge*' were all professional men. The president, Thomas B. Addison, later became the Recorder of the borough, and the secretary was Robert Ashcroft, town clerk from 1852 to 1875. The treasurer, Joseph Livesey, was locally famous as a successful cheesemonger, town councillor, lifelong radical and prominent temperance advocate. The subscriptions were 6s 6d a year, equivalent to almost £17 today, and the aims were "*to facilitate and promote the diffusion of useful knowledge among the operative mechanics and others, inhabitants of Preston and its neighbourhood*". The committee was to consist of twenty-four, of whom fourteen had to be operatives, thus giving some control to the working class members. This rule, however, was altered several years later as it proved impracticable.

A large room was rented in No.21 Cannon Street for £10 a year and was soon arranged for lectures and for a library. Gifts to the new institution included books and instruments worth £429 and £152.3s.0d in cash. Other donations included 800 specimens of natural history, 1,140 books and *"a respectable collection of philosophical instruments and chemical apparatus, together with much useless material"*. In the opening year eighteen lectures were given though only two on *'Electricity'* could be classed as of a scientific nature. Eight on *'Phrenology'* proved to be the most popular. This was the study, popular at the time but now discredited, of examining the shape of a person's skull for assessing character and aptitudes. Classes for *'Chemistry'* and *'English Grammar and Composition'* were held in 1829-30 but they took place in the reading room which proved unsatisfactory. Most popular at the Institution was the library where some 1500 volumes circulated at the rate of 300 a week, *"proof....of the regular and studious habits of the members"*. Membership during the first year was 700.

The number of members fell to 551 in the second year and classes in the Autumn and Winter terms were provided in English Grammar and Composition, Botany, Mechanics and Mechanical Drawing, Architecture and Architectural Drawing, Chemistry and Literary and Philosophical subjects. Of the fourteen lectures given nine were scientific and there were also short courses on Electricity, the Steam Engine and Hydraulics. In no other session before 1850 were so many technical subjects attempted but unfortunately for such an ambitious programme the volunteer teachers were neither competent nor experienced and the lectures were usually unattractively presented. Both the equipment available and the rooms used were unsuitable. These were problems experienced at similar institutions across the country; Preston was by no means alone in this respect.

Despite the comparatively small premises the annual membership averaged over 500 by 1850 but the educational work steadily declined. Classrooms were provided, but only when there was a demand. As the payment of competent teachers could not be afforded, those classes which were held were either taught gratuitously by a member or organised on a *"mutual improvement"* basis. Classes in reading, writing and elementary subjects were not offered and the Institution steadily lost the ordinary working men it had initially sought to attract. Even so, among the 412 members in 1841 there were 85 clerks and shopmen, 76 tradesmen, 17 mechanics, 34 joiners and other operatives, but only 6 factory hands. The secretary complained that there was not a single subscriber among the town's many handloom weavers. Requests to local employers to encourage their workers' membership and to display posters in factories never achieved much success.

The problems facing the Preston Institution were the same as elsewhere. It lacked sound financial backing; working men did not like the lectures and classes that had to be provided to attract members; the quality of the teachers was usually unsatisfactory; most of the courses were inappropriate and unsystematic and after a long day at work most people were too tired to wash and get suitably dressed to attend. Probably the most important reason was the generally defective education of the working classes which prevented them benefiting from what was available. Between 1839 and 1841 some 40% of men and 65% of women married or witnessing marriages in Lancashire and Cheshire could not sign their names. Nevertheless the Preston committee always felt that improved premises would solve most of the problems.

The first attempt to start a fund for a new building was made in 1840 when an exhibition at the Corn Exchange raised £280. In 1842 a legacy of £100 and a grant of £250 from the Town Council enabled the purchase of a plot of land opposite the top of Avenham Walks. The foundation stone was laid in 1846 and the Institution's new building was eventually opened in October 1849 at a total cost, inclusive of fittings, of £6000. The main storey had a large library, a spacious reading room, ante-rooms, committee rooms and a lecture theatre with a gallery capable of holding 600 people. In the basement were offices and several good classrooms. The building became known as the *Avenham Institution* and is still used by the University.

In the years after 1850 the steady improvements in elementary education and the provision of government-sponsored incentives and examinations in art and sciences enabled the Institution to employ better teachers and provide worthwhile courses. Lack of funds, however, continued to be the main problem until it was given a bequest of £70,000 by the trustees of the will of Edmund Robert Harris who had died in 1877. As a result the future progress of technical and higher education in Preston was assured. The Institution retained the same name until 1882 but from then until 1956 was known as the *Harris Institute*, to 1973 as the *Harris College of Further Education*, until 1984 as the *Preston Polytechnic* and eight years later as the *Lancashire Polytechnic*. By 1992 the former *Institution for the Diffusion of Knowledge* at No.23 Cannon Street had developed into the *University of Central Lancashire*.

THE HISTORY OF FARRINGDON PARK.

David Hindle

Childhood memories of Preston's parks include the natural amphitheatre of Avenham Park, where I took part the Preston Guilds of 1952 and 1992, to our local park at Ribbleton, with its very 'cool', open air swimming baths. My dad once told me that he believed there used to a zoo on a Preston park and while I recalled that Miller and Moor Parks each had aviaries there were no smelly bear pits or exotic animals. The enigma was compounded by brown and white corporation buses displaying *'Farringdon Park'*, on their direction indicator and terminating near a wooded dingle, with an apology for a gorge crossed by a footbridge linking two housing estates. Hardly a show-stopping park! In my quest to find out more about the origins of Preston's entertainment venues I have discovered that Farringdon Park was once a Victorian gem known as the *Preston Pleasure Gardens* incorporating a zoological garden and picturesque landscaped woodland area called *'The Dingle'* The park also became known as *'Vauxhall Park'*. Before the building of today's housing estates in the 1930s it was the venue for *Preston Speedway Ltd.* Gone but not entirely forgotten, Preston's lost park has a fascinating history.

During the last years of the 17th century the Farringtons of Farrington Hall, Ribbleton, sold their estate to the Heskeths of Rufford. In 1855 Preston's cemetery became a feature of the landscape when Sir Thomas Hesketh sold over 40 acres and the newly consecrated ground paid host to its first interment. Thereafter the remaining 43 acres of the estate were in use as a nursery managed by James Huddart. According to *Hewitson's History of Preston*, (1883) this land was sold in 1875 to the *Preston Nursery and Preston Pleasure Gardens Company, Ltd.* ' After being purchased by the company they were entirely remodelled; the natural advantages of the site were developed, walks were laid out and the *'Dingle'* was rendered accessible to the public. A large conservatory, 120' by 30', and numerous greenhouses, were erected, and a neat entrance lodge was built'. The gardens were opened for entertainment in 1877; *'a large dancing platform and other accessories being provided'*

Their first venture, which had been intended as an open air show, was ruined by wet weather. In July, 1878, the Royal Horticultural Society held a grand provincial show in the grounds. Though a financial failure, it was considered to be one of the finest horticultural exhibitions ever held in the provinces. A large section of the nursery was sold at auction in November 1880. The pleasure gardens were popular after the 1882 Preston Guild and thousands were attracted from far and wide by advertising propaganda, *'tram cars from all the railway platforms, direct to the gates, every few minutes'.* A lodge and handsome entrance gates to the pleasure paradise were situated at the eastern terminus of the Preston tramway system on New Hall Lane. Once through the gates the public could enjoy walks in *'the Dingle'* along-side a stream and waterfall, dance on the open air platform next to the dancing pavilion and refreshment rooms, play football or cycle race around the perimeter of the football pitch. On Sunday, 20th August, 1884 the accounts show an attendance of 2,853 with gate money of £36.2.9d.

Talk about - *'if you go down to the woods today your in for a big surprise'!* One feature probably came as a complete surprise to an unsuspecting public, who now got their first glimpse of strange and exotic animals, for here was Preston's first and last zoological garden, managed, in 1884, by the distinguished Norfolk writer and naturalist, Arthur C. Patterson. Over 200 hundred birds and animals representing 100 species were accommodated, ranging from a toucan to a seal and over five species of monkey. The accounts of the zoo and weekly reports of animal arrivals and departures by its head keeper during 1884 make fascinating reading. Indeed records suggest the survival rate was pretty abysmal at Preston Zoo:

Week ending 27th August: 'Gentlemen, The following deaths have occurred since last report, 1 toucan, suffering from swollen eye and cold for weeks past. This is the bird so addicted to fits on its arrival; one large cockatoo - of asthma and one half-moon parakeet, presumably of inflammation of lungs'.

w/e July, 31st: Deaths - One marmozette monkey, one piping crow; Arrivals - 2 Jackass birds, one eagle owl, one barn owl, one silver pheasant.

w/e October, 8th: Deaths - one seal been dying for weeks past - very likely since its incarceration. On opening stomach I found a quantity of thread-worms. Would advise company to waste no more money over seals; the experience of last year, (when several died) and of this one dying this (after lasting a season) would go to prove that something, either in the place itself, or requirements is inadequate. I would advise too that nothing be put in that 'hole' for several reasons, needless to state! The sum value of one seal would purchase two fallow deer and perhaps a pair of red deer and these would cost but a fraction of the keep of one seal".

Overall it seemed that the writing was on the wall not only for the wretched seal confined to its inglorious hole but also for the zoological aspect of the pleasure gardens. When the zoo closed in 1885, Arthur Patterson moved back to Yarmouth and made reference to his experiences at Preston Zoo in his book, *'Nature in Eastern Norfolk'.* *"In January, 1884, I tried to better my position by undertaking the management of a small zoo in Lancashire. I tried to bring order out of chaos, and succeeded; but there was so much mismanagement among the directors and their friends - their friends especially - that the affair collapsed, and in 1885 I found myself stranded in Yarmouth again, with an empty purse".*

Beryl Tooley wrote about her great grand-father in her book, *'John Knowlittle'* - Patterson's pseudonym - in which she records: *"The zoo had been mismanaged for some time, and having become very run down, Arthur's job was to try to get it back into some sort of order. By careful dieting and sanitary methods, he reduced the loss of seven animals a week to an average of one death per month. Arthur made a feature of feeding the seals and monkeys, and in part of the winter-garden - a large, glass building in which grew trees - he introduced white herons, cockatoos, peafowl and doves and called it, The Great White Aviary. He constructed other aviaries in the building, decorated the monkey cages with trapeze and added to the zoo a collection of Barbary apes, a flock of demoiselle cranes, a Mexican tiger-cat, Coali Mundi and a fox. Arthur took an assistant - John 'Menagerie Jack' Evers - a hard working lad who paid his mother's rent by breeding and selling guinea pigs and rabbits. John took over as keeper when Arthur left in 1884 until the zoo closed down in 1885 and he obtained work in Manchester".*

1885, saw yet another chapter in the history of Preston Pleasure Gardens, when they were leased by agent Thomas Shuttleworth on behalf of the lessor Thomas Horrocks Miller, of Poulton-le-Fylde to Messrs Janet, James and William Oakey of Preston. A press release at the time stated that *"Several additional improvements have been made. The most important of these is the warming of the new dancing pavilion with hot water making it comfortable at all times. The arrangements both in the zoological and horticultural departments are such as are done to increase the pleasures and profit of all visitors. Messrs J.J. & W. Oakey will personally supervise the management".*

The life of the park after its original opening in 1877 was short-lived and in 1889 it was sold. In 1904 *Barrett's Preston Directory,* referred to the old leisure venue as *'Farringdon Park',* proclaiming it to be, *'the most charming resort for extensive open air gatherings in north-east Lancashire'* incorporating a new half-mile trotting track and racecourse, football ground and dancing pavilion'. In 1925 Preston Grasshopper's

Rugby Club became tenants and four years later a motor cycle syndicate took out a sub-tenancy from the rugby club. For about three seasons Preston Speedways Ltd. played host to many international riders of great repute. The speedway attracted spectators of up to 14,000 and there were several fatal accidents. Celebrities of the dirt track once included George Formby. Winning a challenge race while riding a two stroke machine his time for the three laps of 3/4.of a mile was 1 minute 45 seconds. One way or another it certainly '*turned out nice again*', for George. The film title bearing his famous catch-phrase, was actually shot on location just a mile or so away at Horrocks Crewdson and Co. The firm placed their huge textile mill at the film maker's disposal, giving the workers the week off and some of them an opportunity to become extras in the film.

This legendary name of Horrocks epitomised 'King Cotton' when Preston's industrial base once had up to 50% of the workforce employed in the cotton industry. Although the speedway was very popular its opening in 1929 coincided with widespread unemployment. Economic depression and widespread deprivation meant that people could not afford to catch a tram or pay the 1/- admission fee and by 1932 Preston Speedway faced bankruptcy. Alas, the former glories of Preston Pleasure Gardens and later Farringdon Park slipped into the annals of history. The present-day parameters of the former 44 acre park today comprises Farringdon Park housing estate, though the woodland legacy remains.

In recent years attempts have been made to restore '*The Dingle*' to some of its former glory. Stone steps and a fish pond have been uncovered by job-creation schemes and in May, 1977, to mark the centenary of the opening of the Pleasure Gardens in 1877, hundreds of people turned up to see the Mayor of Preston, Councillor Harold Parker, perform a reopening ceremony. By 1981 a plaque left by the workers as a memorial to their operation clean-up had been smashed by vandals. The stream had been blocked by the remains of old cars and trees vandalised. One cannot help but think that the efforts of those who endeavoured to transform the face of Preston's lost park, sadly, seem to have been in vain.

UNDERNEATH THE ARCHES - 1902

The Stanley Street Arch, Preston Guild, 1902

This triumphal arch, erected in the days before the opening of Preston Guild Merchant in 1902, was built of bales of cotton, the raw material that had given 19th century Preston its prosperity. It was fitting that Stanley Street had been selected for such arch because less than a hundred yards beyond on the right was the entrance to the Yard Works, the centre of the mighty cotton empire, established by John Horrocks in 1791. Over on the left is a wall which enclosed the Old Courthouse of 1829, now the Museum of Lancashire, and, seen faintly through the arch near the corner of New Hall Lane the former Militia Barracks Store House, built in 1854 but now demolished.

The Fishergate Arch, Preston Guild, 1902

Visitors to the Preston Guild celebrations of 1902 passed through magnificent triumphal welcoming arches on the town's (or is it city's?) main roads approaching the centre. The Fishergate arch, in the Roman style, stood astride the road near Fishergate Baptist Church. To the left is the entrance arcade of the former Theatre Royal where a a performance of Gilbert and Sullivan's *"Yeoman of the Guard"* was being shown. The legend *"Stanley for Ever"* relates to the former election cry of supporters of the fourteenth Earl of Derby, M.P. for Preston up to 1830 when he was defeated by Henry *"Orator"* Hunt. The Earl of Derby, his descendant, was Guild Mayor of Preston in 1902.

Adelphi Street Arch, Preston Guild, 1902

This triumphal arch, in the Moorish style, stood at the junction of Adelphi Street and Victoria Street. Flanking the arch along the roofline are the advertising boards of Michael Costello's Victoria Hotel which was situated at 99, Adelphi Street. By the time the photographer had set up his camera in the street, groups of well-dressed locals including, to the right of the arch, two gentlemen dressed in the official robes of the guild, have come together to be recorded as part of history.

The Garstang Road Arch, Preston Guild, 1902

This huge triumphal arch is emblazoned with the words *"Long live our King and Queen"*, only the first letters of each word being visible in the photograph. It appears to have been situated near the entrance gates of Moor Park. Interestingly, it is covered with sections of bark from trees, which may be an allusion to the historic Forest of Fulwood which existed in Medieval times. Only a horse and trap and a solitary cyclist use the road; the days of the petrol engine was yet to come.

These four 1902 photos were loaned by Miss I. Dark and
captioned by Stephen Sartin

A SOCIAL HISTORY OF PRESTON'S POPULAR ENTERTAINMENT INDUSTRY

David Hindle

The Carleton, the Cosy, Fleckie Bennetts, Savoy, Star, Lido, Plaza, Palladium, Rialto, Guild, Ritz, Kings' Palace and the *Royal Hippodrome* to name but a few! In remembering the cinemas and theatres of my youth I am reminded that Preston provides a wonderful opportunity to study the developments to the popular entertainment industry in a northern textile town, reflecting social change during the 19th and 20th Centuries. Preston once had up to five theatres and twenty two cinemas.

The persona of the music hall star was in complete contrast to the nature of entertainment offered at the town's class-conscious *Theatre Royal* built in 1802. The theatre eventually became an A.B.C. Cinema and was demolished in 1955. Nowadays it seems almost beyond belief that on the site of *Etam's* Fishergate store great exponents of culture, including such names as Franz Lizst, Niccolo Paganni and Charles Dickens had delighted audiences during the first half of the 19th Century.

The era of the travelling circus and menagerie is exemplified by a visit to Preston of *Atkin's Royal Menagerie*, which came to the market place on the 27th March, 1824. The propaganda in the *Preston Chronicle* reported on what sounded like the equivalent of Blackpool's 'Golden Mile'. *There were 'extraordinary scenes of affection for the performing male lion and the beautiful Bengal tigress in the same cage. The noble lioness has again whelped two cubs - the cubs, which are now living in perfect health, are so tame and inoffensive that they may be handled and caressed with the same ease and safety as a lap dog'. And as for that 'truly singular and most wonderful animal, the Aurochos, - 'words can only convey the two long horns growing from its forehead in a form peculiar to no other animal' This species is described as a European wild ox and is* **now extinct.**
By contrast one could see a pair of those extraordinary rare birds, 'the pelicans of the wilderness - the only two in the United Kingdoms'. The bizarre advertising gave plen-

ty of warning regarding admittance for unwary, curious Prestonians. *"Admittance ladies and gentlemen 1s, servants and children 6d. feeding time half past nine o clock, 2s"*.

In 1882 the Preston's music halls and theatres included *'The Theatre Royal'*, the brand new *'Gaiety Palace of Varieties'* (later the *'Princes Theatre'*) and the 3,500 capacity Public Hall. Public house concert rooms were in effect early music halls and included taverns at the *Clarence Hotel*, Grimshaw Street, the *George and King Head Inns,* Friargate, and the *Sun Inn,* Mein Spirit Weind, The meaning of *traditional music hall* is distorted, though in Preston the concept was probably fulfilled with the style of entertainment on offer at the taverns and early theatres, where audience participation became part of the performance.

Preston's population of lower wage earning increased from 70,000 in 1851 to 91,500 by 1881. They took up the call of *"lets all go to the music hall"*. With the coming of the railways around 1840 there was an increased demand for leisure and entertainment which impacted on theatre audiences. Popular entertainment was influenced by the social considerations of the day: the drink trade and temperance, morals and religion, gender issues and the growing suffragette movement, patterns of employment, housing and living conditions, wartime and political considerations.

The commodious Edwardian variety theatres of Preston presented, for the first time, *'Twice Nightly'* performances and a matinee, making the performances more attractive to women. They were run by commercial theatre managements such as the Manchester based Broadhead family, who engaged artists on what was affectionately known as *'the bread and butter circuit'*. The family owned two theatres in Preston and engaged music hall acts. There were confrontations with the licensing authorities over the provision of new theatres. However, the public house venues and the Victorian *'Gaiety Theatre'* (1888) had set the foundations for the new architecturally designed people's emporia:- Broadhead's Edwardian *Royal Hippodrome* (1905), *Kings' Palace Theatre* (1913) and Edwin Bush's superb *Empire Theatre* on Church Street (1911). The splendid new theatres were welcomed by Prestonians and prevailed upon the town's social history by presenting almost half a century of popular entertainment.

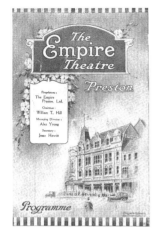

The Empire Theatre is nicely illustrated on the front of this 1924 theatre programme featuring the Raynor Repertoire Company.

The new halls, with beautiful plaster work, boxes for the more affluent, and several tiers ascending to the roof had audience capacities between 1000 and 2500 people. Traditional music hall was staged at Preston's *Empire* and the Broadhead's *Royal Hippodrome* and *Kings' Palace* theatres Typical of what was on offer were novelty acts including exponents of origami, jugglers, magicians, ventriloquists, comics, singers and even performing dogs and monkeys.

The variety theatres, which were still colloquially referred to as '*music halls*' until the mid 20th century, featured legendary names treading the boards of Preston's illustrious halls. Artists such as Harry Lauder with his Scottish origins and Marie Lloyd - the original '*good time girl*'. Marie Lloyd was one of the last of the classic music hall acts who so epitomised the era, appearing at the *Hippodrome* in 1911. Typically, she would have engendered a tremendous rapport between artist and audience with '*oh Mr. Porter*' and '*my old man said follow the band and don't dilly dally on the way*' and her repertoire of double meaning songs. She was one of the most famous and controversial women of the era.

The majority of Preston's theatres had been built towards the end of the music hall boom which began in the mid 1800s and lasted until the outbreak of World War 1. Around the time of the Great War, variety theatres began to feature ragtime, reviews, opera, musical comedy and drama to meet the changing tastes of audiences ranging from the working class to the bourgeois. However, variety was far from dead Even the north/south divide was influenced by the doctrines of moral and political ideologies of the archetypal northerner but nevertheless, some performers, like George Formby, began to enjoy success in London. One performer who regularly played the Preston theatres was Jim Tattersall's ventriloquist's act known as

"*Tattersall and Jerry*". It became typical of 20th Century Music Hall style in Preston during the period. He played both the *Kings' Palace* and *Royal Hippodrome* where he was able to interact with his audiences.

At both the *Hippodrome* and the *Palace* there had been a resurgence of interest in variety during the 1930/40s and topping the bill at that time were such household names as Frank Randle, Norman Evans, Richard Tauber, Joseph Locke, John Mills, Norman Evans, Gracie Fields, a very young Shirley Bassey and the famous Preston Repertory Group known as the *Salberg Players* in which Leonard Rossiter was an unknown player learning his trade. Frank Randle was one of the greatest music hall entertainers of his time. He was godfather to another Preston performer who started her career at the *Hippodrome* with the *Salberg Players* in 1951. Janet Munro was the daughter of theatre impresario Alex Munro and they used to live at No, 45, the Boulevard, Preston, before Janet became a very famous Disney film star. Sadly, Janet died in December, 1972, at the age of 38. Many of her movies were shown in Preston's cinemas during the 1960/70s, but alas, they too are no more.

Janet Munro starred opposite Tommy Steel in the film, 'Tommy the Toreador' and is shown here on location

Throughout the first half of the 20th century the demise of music hall was influenced by the advent of cinematograph performances. In 1915 the palatial *Palladium* cinema on Church Street became Preston's first purpose built-cinema The early cinema impresarios in Preston who played a key role in cinema development included Will Onda who perpetuated the national trend of converting buildings such as churches and breweries into cinemas including the opening of Preston's first cinema in 1908 which was situated on North Road. Reflecting the age of sobriety it was called the *Temperance Hall* with 800 seats. The cinema culture of the period was at first epitomised by silent films, and it was only at the beginning of the 1930s that the first talkies featured. Local names for cinemas were not uncommon and another Will Onda cinema, the *Picturedrome* was also known as the *'Ranch House'* because it specialised in showing westerns.

A succession of managers began to follow Onda and cinemas expanded significantly during the 1920s. Social precedents for the day demanded double seats for courting couples. Cinemas had a major part to play in blossoming romances. This aspect of social history doubtless figured in the mating customs of a couple of generations and was only interrupted by the over zealous usherettes flashing their torches on the back rows.

There were some marvellous *flea pits* in Preston. *'Fleckie Bennett'*, managed the *Dominion Electric Cinema* - a real *'laugh and scratch'*, and close by his arch rival Alfred Wiles opened the *Cosy* cinema in a converted chapel in 1921. He was assisted by *'chucker out'* and doorman, Elijah Waddilove who also made home made lemonade which he sold in jam jars at one halfpenny for a 1lb jar and one penny for a 2lb jar. Admission to the *Cosy* for children was one penny or an empty jam jar. On Saturdays a talent show was staged for locals who would attempt to sing, whistle in tune or dance in their new clogs. - the prize, a jar of Elijah's lemonade and free admission!!

With the coming of the *'talkies'* in 1929 the hey day of cinemas was enjoyed in sumptuous and proud venues. The *Empire Music Hall's* safety curtain made way for a silver screen in 1930. In several Preston theatres including, the *Empire, Princes, Kings' Palace* and the splendid *New Victoria* a combination of both cinema and live theatre was offered to patrons. The art deco *New Victoria* was built as a hybrid venue with a large stage, orchestra pit and a mighty *Wurlitzer* organ which emerged from the murky depths of the stage during the interval. It was latterly converted and became a full time cinema.

By contrast to the *'New Vic'*. at the *'Savoy'* pandemonium was frequent during the pregnant pauses between reels or when the projector broke down. The manager (Ernie) drove the fastest cinema in the west of Preston and his long pole had several uses including fishing for the primitive lights, not to mention sorting out us kids with our bags of parched peas. At the rather posh *Ritz Cinema* the performances were continuous rather than twice nightly. I queued for what seemed like hours along corridors and into Church Street to see the main feature film from the middle onwards then the supporting film, then the adverts, news and trailers before getting to the point at which I came in and then sometimes sitting through it all again to get my own back!

The hey day of Preston's cinemas and theatres was at an end during the 1950s when they succumbed to changes in youth culture and popular taste caused by television. Audience taste had led to the demise of music hall and the writing was on the wall for commercial theatre. Managerial opportunism and male prurience even secured a place for the display of nude women on stage including the famous *'Jane'* who strutted her stuff while posing motionless on stage at the *Palace*. In later years John Osborne wrote, *"The Music Hall is dying and with it a significant part of England"*. People were happier to go for a game of Bingo, enjoy a pint in a night-club with live entertainment or dance the night away at the local *'Mecca'* and all these functions were provided in an increasing number of old cinemas and theatres. Others became garages, supermarkets, or were simply demolished. It is a sign of the times and perhaps a link with Preston's illustrious history of entertainment that many of Janet Munro's movies can now be seen on video and DVD. The *Royal Hippodrome*, where she started her career itself witnessed the very last curtain call when a shower of bricks and debris descended across the once proud proscenium and with it the last vestige of this particular chapter of history disappeared into oblivion.

Q. What ails Preston? A. Ale ails Preston

In 1910, John Henry Musk, a prominent Temperance worker, made some calculations about the amount of money spent on drink in his home town. Based upon figures given for the nation's spending on alcohol, Mr Musk, who lived at "Bentcliffe", Fulwood, calculated that, based on Preston's population of 118,000 and set against the national average of £3/8/11d for every man, woman and child, Prestonians must spend £406,650. He realised that many would not be able to perceive the enormity of that sum, so he broke it down to show that Preston's drink bill for the previous year would pay for:-

	£
2000 House rents, at £18 per annum	36,000
2000 Suites of furniture, at £15	30,000
20,000 Suits of clothes, at £3	60,000
20,000 Hats, at 3s	3,000
20,000 Pairs of men's boots, at 15s	15,000
40,000 Pairs of men's hose, at 1s	2,000
40,000 Mens shirts at 4s	8,000
20,000 Women's dresses at £2	40,000
20,000 Women's hats, at 10s	10,000
20,000 Pairs of women's boots, at 10s	10,000
20,000 Parcels of underclothing, at 20s	20,000
20,000 Boys and girls outfits, at 30s	30,000
20,000 Pairs of blankets, at 20s	20,000
20,000 Counterpanes at 10s	10,000
20,000 Pairs of sheets, at 5s	5,000
20,000 Tablecloths at 5s	5,000
20,000 Bags of flour, at 20s	20,000
20,000 Tons of coal, at 18s	18,000
20,000 Grocery parcels, at 20s	20,000
10,000 Families holidays at seaside, at £4	40,000
Donation to Livesey Memorial Hall	3,000
Donation to local charities	1,650
Total	£ 406,650

The market place in 1842.
All the traders under *"the obelisk"* are female.
The shops are owned by people with good old Preston names –
"Cookson" and *"Threlfall"*

Thanks to the Victorian artists, engravers and printers who combined their skills to produce letter headings depicting the premises occupied by a particular firm, we can today see and admire those premises, even though they may have received the attention of the bulldozer which has seen off much of old Preston.

Mr Crane managed to get the Preston Lamb onto his invoices as well as his workshop

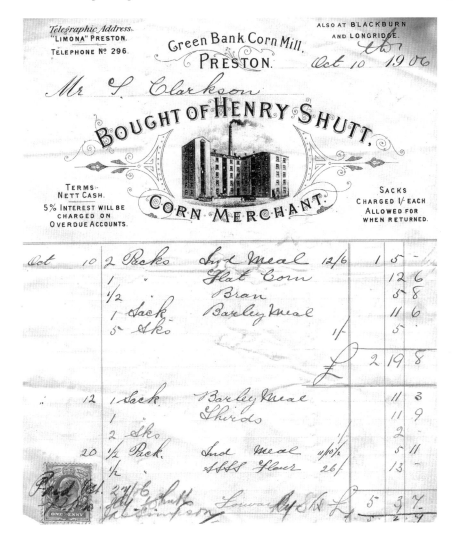

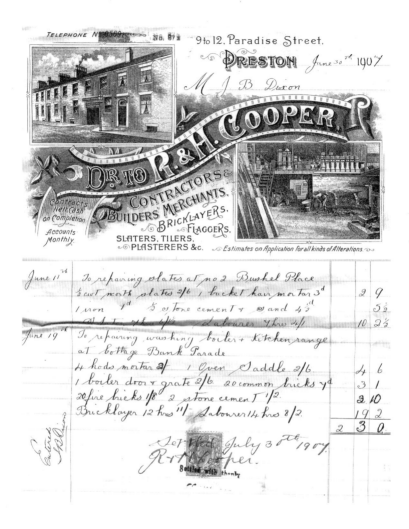

M J B Dixon

Dr. to **R. & H. COOPER,**

CONTRACTORS &
BUILDERS' MERCHANTS,
BRICKLAYERS,
FLAGGERS,
SLATERS, TILERS,
PLASTERERS &c.

Contracts
Nett Cash
on Completion.

Accounts
Monthly.

Estimates on Application for all kinds of Alterations.

June 11th	To repairing slates at no 2 Bushel Place		
	½ cwt north slates 2/6 1 bucket hair mortar 3d	2	9
	1 iron 1d 5 stone cement + sand 4½d		5½
	Slater 7h. 4/5 labourer 7hrs 4/1	10	2½
June 19th	To repairing washing boiler + kitchen range		
	at cottage Bank Parade		
	4 hods mortar 2/ 1 Oven Saddle 2/6	4	6
	1 boiler door + grate 2/6 20 common bricks 7d	3	1
	20 fire bricks 1/8 2 stone cement 1/2.	2	10
	Bricklayer 12 hrs 11/- Labourer 14 hrs 8/2.	19	2
		2 3	0

Settled July 30th 1907
R & H Cooper.

Settled with thanks

To George Arrowsmith Dr.

BUILDERS' MERCHANT, etc.

ESTABLISHED
OVER HALF-A-CENTURY

SPECIALITIES :		SPECIALITIES :
Earle's Portland Cement.		Drain Pipes, Gullies, etc.
HALL'S SANITARY		RED. BUFF & SALT-GLAZED
Washable Distemper.		Chimney Pots.
WHITE, CANE AND SALT		Garden Tiles & Flower Vases.
Glazed Sinks.		PIG TROUGHS AND
PEDESTAL CLOSETS,		CATTLE TROUGHS.
HOPPERS & TRAPS,		
Lavatories.		BLUE STAFFORDSHIRE
ALL KINDS OF TILES		Stable and Facing Brick.
FOR		
Hearths, Walls, Floors,		Channel Tiles,
&c. &c.		&c. &c

ORMSKIRK ROAD, PRESTON, _Sept 30th_ 1901

M_r_ J. Nevett & Son.

Worthington's Estate

July 5	To rep. cement floors, cornice &c				
	at 72 & 74 Fishwick Parade.				
"	R Caton 9 hrs	10½		7	11
"	M Hall 9 "	7		5	3
"	Cement sand, lime & plaster			5	4
				18	6

Oct 7 _Settled_

Estab. 1874.   Tel. No. 46x2.

MOUNT STREET PRINTING WORKS,
(3 DOORS FROM FISHERGATE)

Preston, _June 30_ 1906

Mr Reveley

Dr. to J. CRANE,

General Printer, Bookbinder, etc.

EVERY DESCRIPTION OF PRINTING AND BOOKBINDING EXECUTED PROMPTLY AT
REASONABLE PRICES.

POSTERS— any size.
Handbooks.
Catalogues.
Reports.
Prospectuses.
Programmes.
Circulars.
Delivery Books.
Receipt Books.

Billheads
Memorials
Post Cards
Business
Invitations
Wedding
Memorial
Dance
Prog.
&c.

Estimates Given

BOOKBIND

Apr. 5	100 Bills — £5 Reward			4
	Conviction — illegally taking trout. &c			

PAYMENT OF OPERATIVES IN THE TEMPERANCE HALL PRESTON

The artist from the *Illustrated London News* captured the mood of the striking cotton operatives well in these studies. Few other pictures of Preston show the windmill in full sail. The pictures appeared in the issue on 12th November 1853.

A classic shot of Preston in the late 1800's. We are looking east towards the Town Hall from Chapel Street and Winckley Street. Prominent on the left is the tower of the Preston Gas Company's fine building. J & H Platt, printers and stationers are still in business, though now in Fishergate. As is usual in photos taken in this period, every lad and chap is wearing a cap. - *Perhaps bought at Jackson,s!*

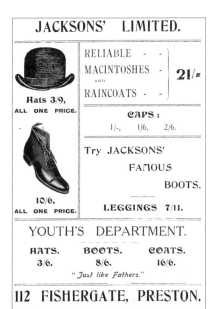
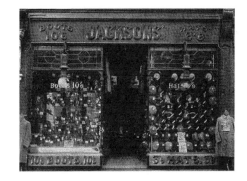

THE RAILWAY HOTEL AND MILLER PARK.

The *Illustrated London News* sent their artist to the 1882 Guild. These are a few of his drawings, which brought national prominence to Preston.

ST. JOHN'S PARISH CHURCH.

THE OLD SHAMBLES.

THE MECHANICS' INSTITUTION.

These two photographs are from an archive relating to *"Preston Harriers"*. This club was formed in 1881 at a meeting held in the *"White Horse Inn"*, Cheapside. The four young girls had just represented the club at a *Northern Counties Amateur Athletic Association* meeting, held at Leigh in 1949. Jean Eastham, Lucy Giddins, Hilda Walmsley, and Alice Higginson, in their *Preston Harriers* vests, ran in the 4x110yds relay event. The four girls were all 16 years of age, and came second, even though the baton was dropped. The other photo shows Jim Woodhouse (wearing spectacles) and Maurice Dean representing the Harrier Walking Section in the *"Manchester to Blackpool Walk"* in 1953. They are being escorted through Lostock Hall by a team of *"groupies"* who supported their Harrier boyfriends, (Marian Wareing on the rear cycle was to marry Maurice). The Walking Section had been going since the club's inception. Today Preston Harriers (one of two Athletic Clubs in Preston) has over four hundred members, but is without a walking section. The club's history is full of champions at levels ranging from Inter-club to National and Olympic- and there are more to come.

(*Photos from Maurice Dean's Collection*).

The flower display on the lamp posts suggest that this photo was taken just prior to the 1952 Guild - on a Thursday (half-day closing) at 5pm. I can't be more precise that that. The photographer is looking up Friargate towards Cheapside and is standing close to the junction with Orchard Street and Bamber's Yard (which is now the entrance to St. George's Shopping Centre). Most of the shops on the right, including the *Boars Head* pub selling Tetley's beers, were demolished to make way for the shopping centre. Greenwood's moved their shop inside the new centre to continue fitting out more generations of Preston's dads and lads with sports jackets, flannels and caps.

The Church of England bishops are under the eye of PC 1757 Freddie Nelson astride *"Colonel"* as they proceed along Church Street towards the parish church. They are passing the New Victoria cinema near to the junction with Lancaster Road and have chosen not to visit the *"iron aisles"* which the photographer has caught on the right during the 1922 Guild.

Cycling was a major activity in the days around the turn of the century and before the Great War. Even so, Mr Cookson diversified by trading also in motor cars and gas mantles in his North Road shop. He hadn't embraced the latest technology - the telephone, by 1908 when he used this photo in an advert.

I REMEMBER PRESTON

I said to myself one day
I must write them down before I grow old
And forget my memories of the town
I came to as a girl.

Library, Guild Hall, ships sailing in from the sea
And a Market glowing with colour
Behind old streets with names
Like Cheapside and Friargate –
These were Preston to me
Back in the far-off Thirties as a newcomer.
Church bells on Sundays, stately Civic processions,
The friends I made, who showed me
The cafes and shops and plushy cinemas
(Then in their heyday)
And Francis Thompson's house,
And Easter egg-rolling, and the Whitsuntide Fair!
And who took me further afield
To see chestnut-candles in Fulwood and Penwortham,
To picnics and parties and Sunday School dances
And ducks on the pond in Moor Park –
Afterwards walking me home
In a misty Midsummer moonlight
Through friendly familiar streets
In a safe and respectable dark!

Preston and people seem very different today,
Only sometimes in, say, Winckley Square
On an April night (just passing through)

I like to imagine the years never happened,
That brought the coming of war, and the Yanks
And the black-out and air-raid warnings
And rationing – that's life as it was before –
And thinking of Preston's long history,
Standing there still
See the ghost of the girl that was me,
Walking lightly with stars in her eyes
Up Fishergate Hill!

This poem was written by Joan Pomfret (Mrs Townsend), who was the daughter of the Preston Borough Librarian. She became a journalist. With several books of poetry to her name during and after the Second World War, Joan ranks amongst the very best Lancashire dialect poets and story tellers. This poem appears by permission of the Lancashire Authors Association, who hold copyright on her work. Joan died in 1993 aged 80 years.

Joan's memories will strike a chord with many Prestonians.

Few photographs exist which show workplaces in the first decade of the twentieth century. Here's the Preston Steam Laundry's ironing room. Although these lasses were on their feet all day, compared with cotton mills these looked like good working condition - airy and well lit. The firm operated in Addison Road but received work at their office in the Miller Arcade. They also cleaned carpets in Wildman Street, and, even though they had a telephone, encouraged customers to send a post card in order that their collecting van might call.

150

Preston AND COUNTY | **Pilot;** ADVERTISER.

[N°. 1525.—VOL. XXX]   SATURDAY, FEBRUARY 25, 1854.   [PRICE 4½d.]

THE PRESTON PILOT : A LEADING LIGHT

Bob Dobson

Not the first Preston newspaper – it was preceded by the 'Preston Journal', the 'Preston Review' and the 'Preston Sentinel' – the 'Preston Pilot' was to become a most important local paper for the town in the reigns of George the Fourth and Victoria.

Started on the first day of 1825 by the printer Lawrence Clarke from his address in Church Street, (though printed in nearby Blue Bell Yard), in appearance it resembled the Sentinel which was also printed by Clarke and which he had started just four years previously.

Big and bold was the Pilot's banner, comprising the Royal, the town's and country's heraldic badges or arms, all surrounded by foliage comprising the rose, shamrock and thistle – perhaps there were no Welsh readers in the town at that time. This decoration also depicted water (the Ribble?) on which was a sailing ship.

The editor concentrated on local news, often set against what was happening in the country at large. Right at the outset, readers were told of the 'Pilot's policy .... *"to place before the enlightened and extensive population a weekly paper that shall breathe the spirit of uncompromising honesty and beam with the light of undeviating truth"*. In political terms, the publishers upheld *"love for our country, faithful and loyal to our King and staunch to the principles of our splendid constitution......(we will) never raise the blush on the cheek of either wife or child"*. True blue Conservatism.

The 'Pilot' prospered before commercial competition from the financially-strong Preston Guardian and Preston Herald forced changes – it became the 'Preston Pilot and County Advertiser' and then the 'Preston Pilot and Lancashire Advertiser', then was published on a Wednesday instead of a Saturday, and for a time was a free paper. There were also changes in the number of pages, reflecting the prosperous years before fortunes turned downhill about 1867. Towards the end, which came in 1886, its four pages sold for three-half-pence.

Lawrence Clarke had founded the Preston Sentinel just after going into business on his own after an apprenticeship under Thomas Walker at Town Hall Corner. He must not have proof-read his own work, for the paper's prospectus gave its name as the 'Preston Centinel'. Oops!

* * * * * *

HIGH-TEC HITS PRESTON

The first photographic illustration to appear in the *"Preston Guardian"* was in the issue of 8th February, 1902. Portraits of Archdeacon Rawstorne, Miss Mary Cross and Mr Shaw the headmaster of the *"Royal Cross Deaf and Dumb School"*, with a classroom scene were shown to illustrate a piece about the laying of the foundation stone by the Earl of Lathom on 1st October.

* * * * * *

PRESTON : THE FACTS, 1682

In 1818 was published a book entitled *"A Brief Description of the Burrough of Preston and its Government and Guild, Originally composed between the years 1682 and 1686, with Occasional Notes by John Taylor".*

Taylor was a *"Preston agriculturist and seedsman".*

Have a look at some of its contents:-

A

BRIEF DESCRIPTION

OF THE

Burrough & Town of Preston.

Climate.

THE BURROUGH OF PRESTON, in Amoundernes, as to the clymate, lyeth in the fifty-fourth degree of latitude, abating some few minutes; this part of the country, especially towards the western or Hibernian ocean, being for the most part a level or flatt-ground, and the ayre of a moderate temperature and healthfull.

Situation.

THIS antient Burrough is very pleasantly seated upon a high or riseing ground, more especially from the south or west; such a situation as the Brittains and Romans in antient time either prefixed or annexed a Dunum or Duno to the names of towns so seated as this Burrough. In those dayes by Ptolemy it was styled Tibo Dunum, or Tigo Dunum,

theeves, and sturdy beggars, and dissolute persons of
no good behaviour, at hard work, under a strict master, with most slender dyet and whipping chear, untill
either the publiq Sessions release them, with a naked
and bloody farwell, and them for transportation or
otherwise be enlarged by the judge & justices of the
peace, their order or els retain them with a continando
for the countrys safety, until a further punishment or
reformation give them enlargement, after a sufficient
'expiation for their crimes.

Boundaries.

THE bondary confining the francheses and libertyes
of this Burrough of Preston, beginneth upon the south
side, at the much famed river of Ribell, at a place
cal'd the washing stood, and from thence ascend up,
easterly, by a little rill or rivulet called the Swill-
brooke, crossing the London road and passing upward
to the head thereof, till you come over against the
town of Fishwick, from which this brooke parteth the
burrough aforesaid; and from thence the bonds pass
to the norward, to the entrance upon Ribleton more,
nere, if not close by, the crosse upon the highway a
little above Ribchester, toward the citty of Yorke;
and from this crosse, passing by the west side of that,
more still norward, through some few closes unto
Eavs brook, and thus it is separated from the village
of Ribleton; upon the east from thence, passing down

to the Eavs brook untill it fallith into the water of
Savock, and thus it is parted from the forest of Full-
wood, and Cadily more; so descending the water
Savok to a certain old ditch which is the bondary be-
twixt Preston and Tulketh; see following that old
ditch southward, by Lancaster-lane, untill you arrive
to Preston marsh, a little west from the Water Milne;
and so following the milne streame westward, after
the north side of the marsh, untill it crosse up southward towards Rible, but following that streame to Rible
water; and so following Rible eastward, by the midst
of that water, untill it come past the boat over against
Preston, to the afore mentioned washing steeds, into
the Swillbrook.

River.

THE first of the aforesaid bondary, leaving Penwortham and Walton in le dale upon the south of the
river Rible, which famed river or estuarium, Ptolemy,
in his dayes, styled Belisamia, which, by the ancient
Brittans had been cal'd   Bel, and since by the
Saxons, Danes, and Normans, named Rible water.
above whose high banks the present Burrough of
Preston is situated, upon an elevated ground, such
a syte, as in the Roman time was cal'd a Dunum
from the British word Dun, ever signifying a town
upon a hill or higher situation, as hath been said
before.

Freeman's Oath.

" You shall swear that you shall bee good and true to our sovereign Lord King Charles 2d, and to his heires and lawfull successors, and you shall bee obedient to the just and good Government of this Burrough of Preston ; and, to the best of your power, you shall maintain and preserve the peace, and all your due franchises thereof; and according to your knowledge and ability, doe and performe all other acts and things as doe belong to a Freeman of this Town to doe.   " So help you God."

ABOUT THE AUTHORS

Shane Byrne is a 21 year old who has just completed a BA (Hons) Degree in History at the University of Central Lancashire, where he has been a student for the past three years. He began his research into the 'new police' in Preston during his third year dissertation. He was educated at Edlington School, several miles outside of his home town of Doncaster.

Steve Collins has been researching the life and works of William Harrison Ainsworth for more than ten years, during which time he completed a PhD on Ainsworth's lifelong friend, the Manchester solicitor, bibliophile and founder of the Chetham Society, James Crossley.

Raymond Clayton is self-employed as a public clock restorer. His hobbies include bell ringing, so through his hobby and his work (which is also a hobby) he visits public buildings and churches throughout the North West. He lives at Hoghton and is a verger at the village parish church.

Bob Dobson is a second-hand book dealer and book publisher. Most of his "Landy Publishing" books have been of Lancashire local history interest. A native of Accrington, he is a retired policeman, living near Blackpool. He has compiled books similar to this one on Accrington, Blackpool and Blackburn, and written "Lancashire Nicknames and Sayings", "Policing in Lancashire", "Concerning Clogs" and edited several anthologies of Lancashire dialect verse. If "A Preston Mixture" is successful, he may produce a follow-up to it, and to this end welcomes contacts from potential contributors.

Stephen Halliwell is a Preston-born, Kirkham-educated retired salesman who has lived in his home town for most of his life. A former chairman of Preston Scientific Society, he joined in the mid-70's because of his ornithological interests and through his membership acquired an interest in a wider range of natural history subjects. He spends his leisure time not only in the County Record Office and the Harris Library researching local and family history, but also in far-flung places such as the Scottish Islands looking at birds, studying the islands' past and trying to conserve their future.

David Hindle was born in Preston in 1944. Since retiring from the Lancashire Constabulary in 1992 he has lectured at Alston Hall and taught part time at Cardinal Newman College, Preston. David is a life long conservationist and ornithologist and has a keen interest in local history. He is the author of two books, "Twice Nightly : An Illustrated History of Entertainment in Preston" and "Grimsargh : The Story of a Lancashire Village". David and his wife Dorothy have lived at Grimsargh since 1997. They have one daughter, Caroline, who lives in London.

Robert Ingham is a retired college librarian. His first post was in the Harris Library. During his career he obtained a teaching qualification and taught English. He has contributed poems to several anthologies and now concerns himself with chairing the Ormskirk Probus Club. The Tom Finney poem contributed reflects the happy times he spent on the Deepdale terraces.

Greta Krpczyk-Oddy – Originally from Rochdale and now living in Penwortham, she is a double graduate of the Open University. She holds a certificate in Local History from Lancaster University and one in Latin for Local History from the University of Manchester. A volunteer at the Harris Museum and Art Gallery in Preston, Greta has for the past five years been assisting the Keeper in Social History in cataloguing and archiving the Harris's large collection of 19th and 20th century glass negatives and photographs. She is currently Vice-Chairman of the Friends of the Harris Committee. Greta is particularly interested in works by late 19th and early 20th century female artists and the WSPU movement in Preston. Greta has had articles on Local History and Art History published and some poetry. She is especially interested in embroidery and design within the field of textile art.

Terry Regan is a native of Blackpool. By day he is a builder, by night a local historian and writer. He has written many articles over the past twenty years or so, numbers of which have appeared in newspapers, magazines and books at home and abroad. He enjoys the research which goes into producing stories, especially if that story concerns Lancashire, his first love. One aspect which intrigues him is the part played by Lancashire during the American Civil War. He is writing a book concerning such matters, the pivotal role of which is occupied by a famous Afro-American.

Marian Roberts was born in Preston and lived here all her life until 2002, when family commitments took her to Norfolk. When her husband died in 1980, Marian developed her interest in her home town's past. She enrolled on a succession of courses at the County Record Office and enveloped herself in researching Winckley Square, its inhabitants and those connected with it. She gave talks on its places in local history and in 1988 saw the publication of her book "The Story of Winckley Square". Other talks on Preston were developed and delivered. Her pride in Preston shines through in correspondence with many old Preston pals.

Christopher Reddington Shaw was born and bred in Preston. A retired building surveyor, he has long been a member of Preston Poets' Society and is a trustee of All Saints C of E Church.

Stephen Sartin is Curator of Art for the Lancashire Museum Service. His knowledge of art, artists and of many facets of Preston's past might be said to be chain-linked to the Harris Free Library, Museum and Art Gallery, where he worked for many years. Stephen has vast experience as a writer and lecturer on art and Preston.

Tom Smith was educated at Preston Catholic College and Liverpool University where he graduated in 1953 and completed his master's degree in 1966. Nine years later he obtained a doctorate in educational history at Leeds University. A schoolmaster, he taught at Preston Catholic College and St. Cuthbert Mayne High school until his retirement. He has written extensively on Catholicism in 19th Century Preston and made a study of the town's Court Leet records. A keen walker, sportsman and life-long North End supporter, he still plays golf regularly and was joint author of "On Fulwood Green ' the history of Preston Golf Club.

Nick Wotherspoon works in the Harris Library. Whilst studying for his degree, he was able to combine his interests in local history and transport heritage when he chose to research the story of the "Bond Minicar" for his final year project. This work continued after the course and resulted in the publication of his book "Lawrie Bond : The Man and the Marque" in 1993 (ISBN 1-870519-16-7). The owner of several classic cars, Nick is also passionately interested in the aviation heritage of Lancashire and has created a popular internet website on this subject.

Derek Wrathall was raised around Whitechapel, Bilsborrow and Myerscough before attending Preston Grammar School. He used to meet Barbara Martin on the school bus - a journey which was to lead to marriage. She was of Tullis stock and when, a few years ago they decided to research the family, Derek learned more about the Tullis' connections with Preston's best buildings. He and Barbara now live in retirement at Keighley.